Shit Happens

A Gift Book of Unlikely Quotes

Shit Happens

By
Buck Tilton

Illustrated By
Joe Kohl

ICS BOOKS, Inc.
Merrillville, IN

Shit Happens
Copyright © 1996 by Buck Tilton
10 9 8 7 6 5 4 3 2 1
All rights reserved, including the right to reproduce this book or portions thereof in any form or by any means, electronic or mechanical, including photocopying, recording, unless authorization is obtained, in writing, from the publisher.
All inquiries should be addressed to ICS Books, Inc., 1370 E. 86th Place, Merrillville, IN 46410
Illustrations Copyrighted © by Joe Kohl
Cover photo: SuperStock

Published by:
ICS BOOKS, Inc.
1370 E. 86th Place
Merrillville, IN 46410
800-541-7323

Printed in the U.S.A.

Library of Congress Cataloging-in-Publication Data
Tilton, Buck .
Shit happens : a gift book of unlikely quotes / by Buck Tilton.
p. cm.
ISBN 1-57034-051-X
1. Defecation --Humor . I Title.
PN6231 . D37T55 1996
394 -- dc20   96-22018
                                                              CIP

Introduction

With etymological roots in Old English words such as *scite* and *scitan* ("to defecate"), akin to the Old High German *scizan* and Old Norse *skita* (both, once again, "to defecate"), altered in Middle English to *shite* and *shiten*, and sometimes shyte, our modern word shit claims a proud if odorous heritage. Despite *Merriam Webster's* proclamation that it's "usually considered vulgar," few words have survived as long as *shit*, and probably no word has proven more useful than *shit*.

As a noun, *shit* can mean excrement or an act of defecation, nonsense, any of several drugs, a worthless or detestable person, an unorganized mess, something appealing (*good shit*), or something unappealing (*bad shit*).

As a verb, *shit* (or *shat*) or *shitting* can mean to defecate in, to attempt to deceive, to treat unfairly, to mess up or just about anything else. The adjective *shitty* (i.e., smelly, unappealing, of inferior quality) has probably been ascribed to more nouns than any other descriptive. Oh shit(!) and No shit(!) may have interrupted more sentences than any other exclamation.

In short, here is a universal word, especially for someone who has trouble remembering a lot of vocabulary. And here, also, is this little book, a printed romp through the linguistic world of *shit*.

Note: For the overly cultured or verbally squeamish, the word *shit* can be substituted almost anywhere in this book with bowel movement, ca-ca, chips, crap, crapola, defecation, doo-doo, droppings, dump, dung, excrement, feces, load, number two, poop, poo-poo, poopy, scat, turd—or just about anything else.

· SHIT HAPPENS ·

· SHIT HAPPENS ·

1. Shit, a noun 1: excrement, 2: an act of defecation 3: nonsense or crap; a verb 1: to defecate in 2: to attempt to deceive. Usually considered vulgar.
   —*Merriam Webster's Dictionary*

· SHIT HAPPENS ·

2. Shit, by any other name, would smell the same.
   —With apologies to Shakespeare

· SHIT HAPPENS ·

3. From where the sun now stands, I will shit no more forever.
—Chief Running Bare, died of fecal impaction, 1879

4. Little birdy in the sky
Dropped some birdshit in my eye,
I'm no baby, I don't cry,
I'm just glad that cows don't fly.
—Semi-famous nursery rhyme

5. It's a shitty day to die.
—Sioux war cry

· SHIT HAPPENS ·

6. Do bears shit in the woods? You bet, but that's not all they do.
   —Sex in the Outdoors, attributed to Smokey

7. Shit on me once, shame on you. Shit on me twice, shame on me.

8. Frankly, Scarlett, I don't give a shit.
   —Rhett Buttler

9. Shit-on-a-shingle, a noun creamed chipped beef on toast, hold the ketchup.

10. As long as wind blows, grass grows and shit stinks.
    —From original Indian treaty repeatedly broken by U.S. Army

11. If it's yellow, let it mellow. If it's brown, flush it down.
    —*Shitter's Guide to Water Conservation*

12. Three things give long life: sleep well, eat light, shit heavy.
    —Old Welsh Proverb

13. When it comes to America's farms, politicians are always stepping in what they're trying to sell us.
    —Political Bullshit Expert

· SHIT HAPPENS ·

14. Sometimes I shits and thinks, and sometimes I jus' shits.
—Old Southern Saying

15. Little Jack Horner sat in a corner,
    Eating his Christmas pie,
    He stuck in his thumb, and pulled out a plum, and said
    Shit, I thought it was cherry!
    —Famous Pre-censorship Nursery Rhyme

16. Shit-list, a noun an imaginary roster of everyone you're not very fond of.

17. It was the best of times to shit, it was the worst of times to shit.
    —*A Tale of Two Shitties*

18. Home, home on the range, where the deer and the antelope shit.
—Failed first attempt at early American songwriting

19. Don't let them tear that little brown shithouse down, for there's not another like it in the country or the town.
—Famous song altered just a bit shortly before release

20. Take a shit? Who wants to take a shit? "Leave a shit" sounds more reasonable to me.
—George Carlin

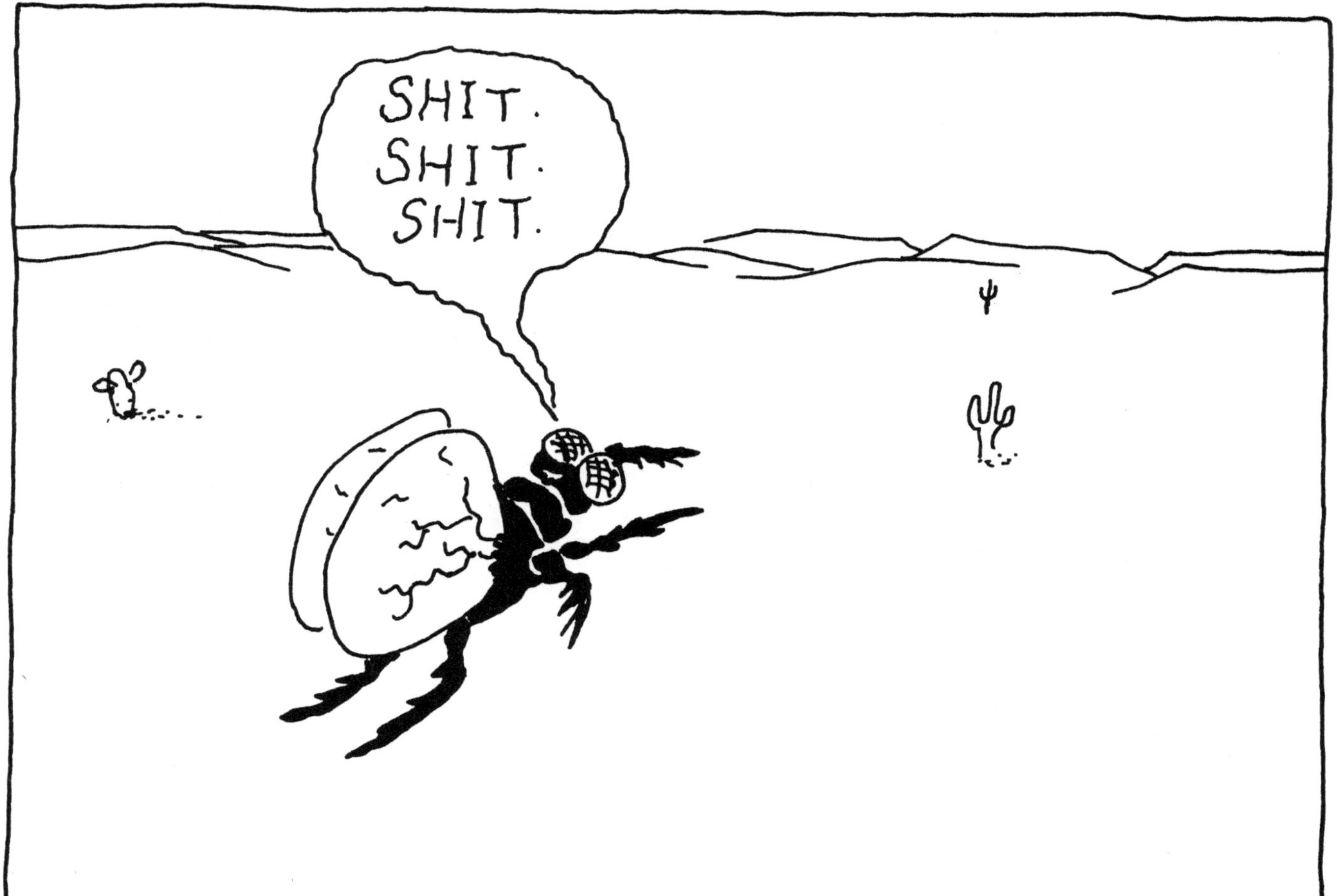
SHIT. SHIT. SHIT.

21. Man shall not live by bread alone, but by every shit that follows the bread.
    —The Gospel According to Shit 2:10
    —Anthropomorphic metaphor

22. Take only pictures, leave only shit.
    —Original motto of the Sierra Club

23. If Thomas Crapper invented the flushing toilet, who invented the shithouse?

24. A shit in time saves underwear.

25. A good shit in the morning is worth two in the evening.
 —Old English Proverb

26. To a Hindu: this shit has happened before.

27. Once you get your shit together, what do you do with it?

28. Oh, give me a home where the buffalo roam, and I'll show you a real shitty house.

29. Diarrhea is when a good shit has more appeal than good sex.

· SHIT HAPPENS ·

30. As dog returns to smell his shit, so the owner steps in it.
—Kung Fushoe

31. A man with diarrhea thinks everyone's happy who shits regularly.
    —Ancient Phoenician Proverb

32. To avoid sickness, eat less. To prolong life, shit more.
    —Ancient Chinese Proverb

33. Shitting is the great equalizer of all men.
    —*The Forgotten Words of Aristotle*

34. When your ideas turn out to be shitty, destroy all evidence that it was your idea.
    —Lickert's Second Lesson

35. A shitty poem:
In days of old, when knights were bold,
And toilets not invented,
They left their load along the road,
And walked off well-contented.

36. Piece of shit, an expression 1: something of inferior quality
2: someone of inferior quality

37. No one will remember your nice ideas, but everyone will remember your shitty ones.
—Lickert's Third Lesson

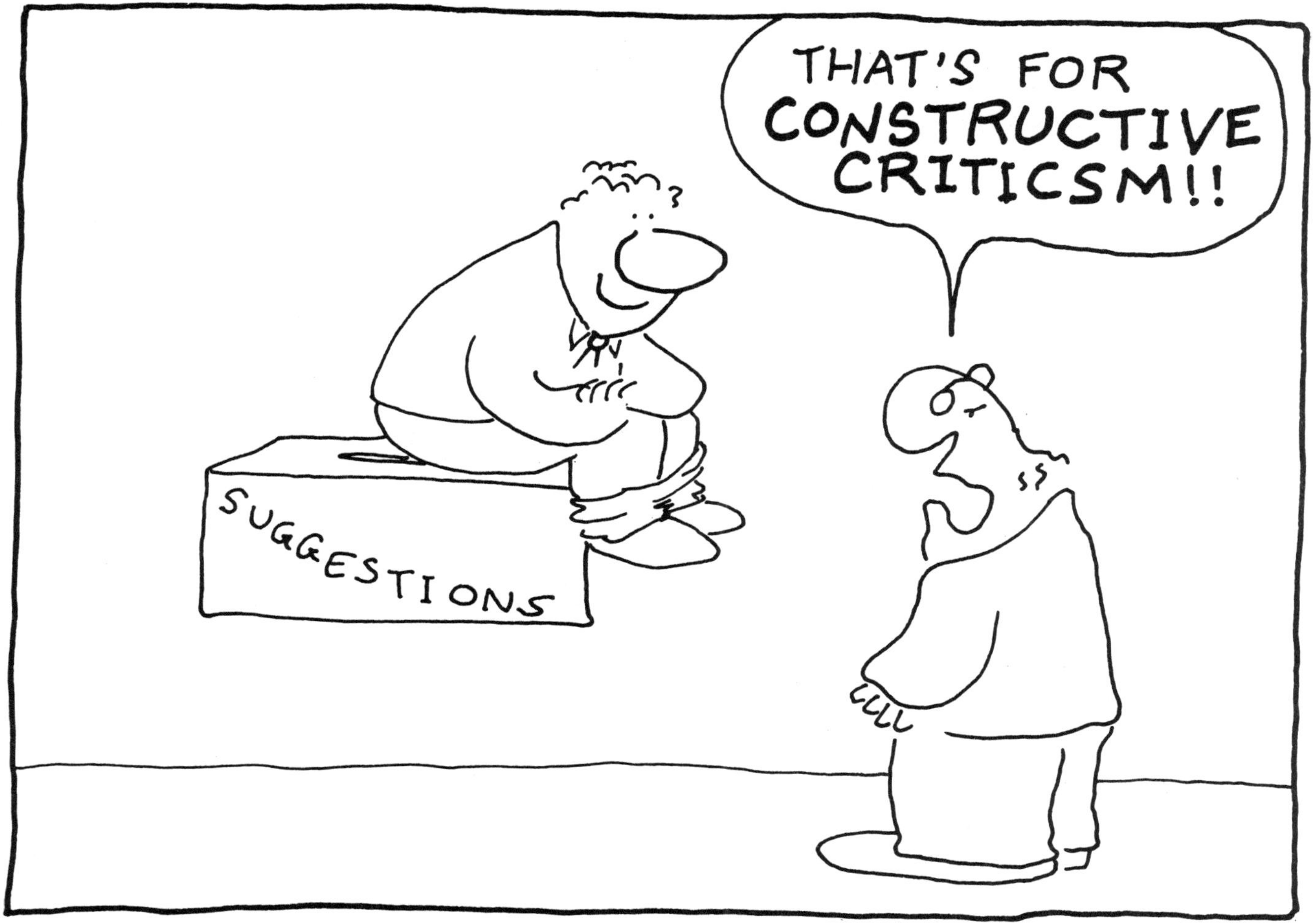
THAT'S FOR CONSTRUCTIVE CRITICSM!!
SUGGESTIONS

·SHIT HAPPENS·

38. Just because you're not paranoid doesn't mean you're not shitting wrong.
   —Union of American Psychotherapists

39. A good shit is like a slight attack of apoplexy.
   —Democritus, sort of

40. International shit guideline:
   In Islamic cultures, since one eats with the right hand, one must wipe with the left. Offering the wrong hand to shake is punishable by death.

41. To avoid shits that smell, one must avoid eating.
    —Guiding directive of the short-lived Anti-smelly Shit Society (ASS)

42. The family that shits together probably has other problems, too.
    —American Union of Psychotherapists

43. To a Buddhist: if shit happens, it really isn't shit.

44. Our need to shit is several millions of years older than our intelligence.

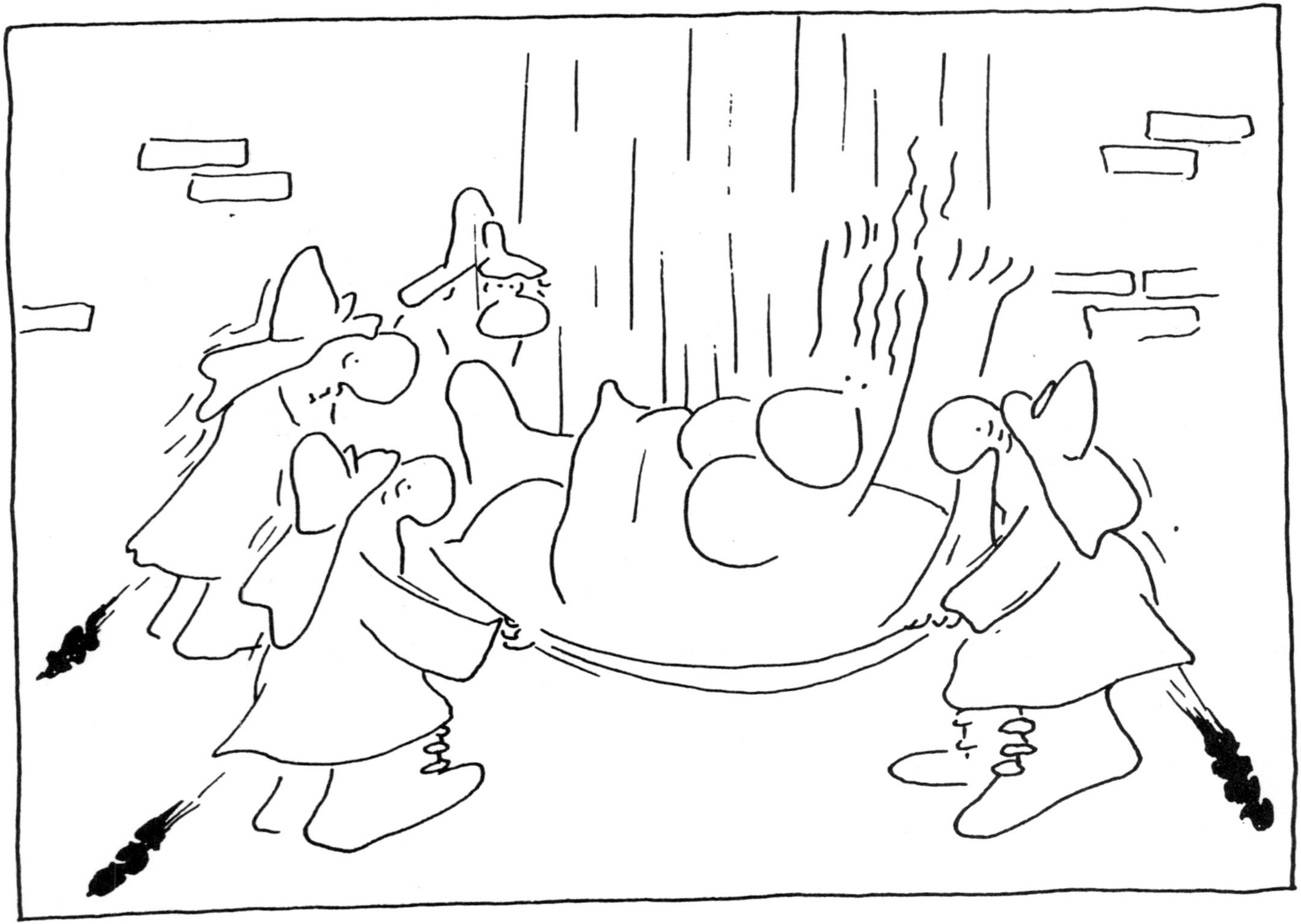

45. Roses are red, violets are blue, your shit stinks, and so do you.
   —St. Valentine to his executioner . . . and the idea caught on

46. You can't make a silk purse out of a sow's ear, but you can make a shit-bag out of anything.

47. Shit-for-brains a noun someone not as smart as you

48. A good shit, like death, requires privacy.
   —*Articles of the Good Shit Club*, Number One

· SHIT HAPPENS ·

49. You never have to shit at a convenient time.
—Murphy's Shit Law

50. Never go to a proctologist whose shitter is down the hall.
—*Advice to the Anally Retentive*

51. There's always a floater left when you flush your shit down a neighbor's toilet.
—Commentary on the Corollary to Murphy's Shit Law

· SHIT HAPPENS ·

52. People who live in glass houses should shit in the basement.

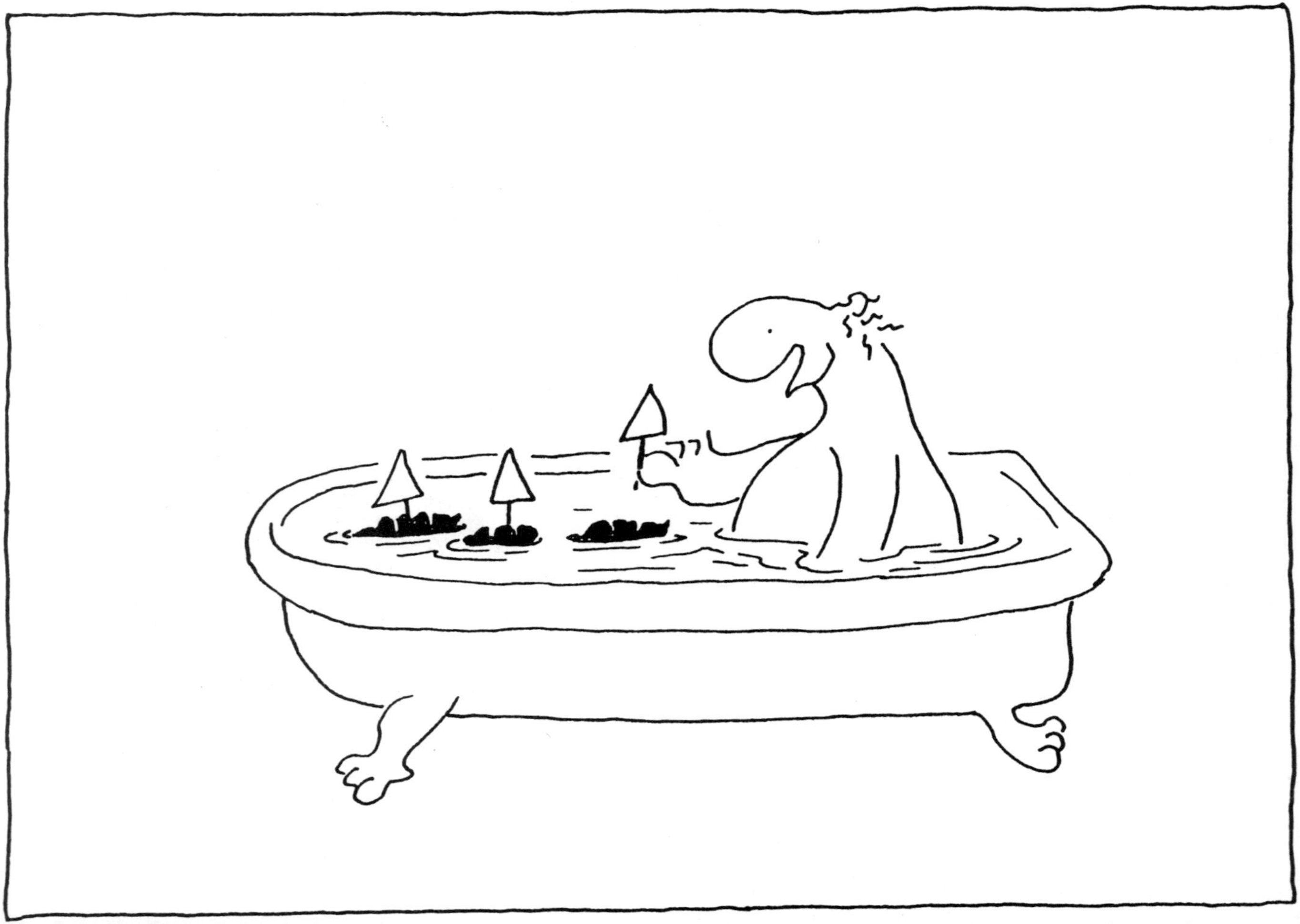

53. One more shit, Martha, and my butt's gonna freeze right off!
    —*The Unpublished Letters of George Washington at
    Valley Forge*

54. Nature has given us two ears and two eyes, but only one asshole. Moral: listen twice, look twice, but when you gotta take a shit, go!

55. Finesse at shitting in the woods—or anywhere else, for that matter—is not come by instinctively.
    —*How to Shit in the Woods*

· SHIT HAPPENS ·

56. Shitter, a noun 1: someone who shits 2: something someone shits into 3: a bad place to be during an earthquake

57. If you think shitting has become boring:
    A. Try it without dropping your pants.
    B. Do it in another room, say, the living room.
    C. Invite a guest to watch.
    D. Consult a psychoanalyst.

58. Bowels are a guest-chamber for shit in the healthy, and for the constipated, a prison.
    —Francis Bacon

· SHIT HAPPENS ·

59. To a Taoist, shit happens.

· SHIT HAPPENS ·

60. A good shit is nature's reward for being in harmony with her laws.
    —*Articles of the Good Shit Club*, Number Two

61. I, for one, know of no sweeter sight for a man's eyes than his own shit.
    —Homer Guile, founder and first president, Good Shit Club

62. Shit-work, a noun 1: work you're stuck with that no one else wants to do 2: writing a book about shit

· SHIT HAPPENS ·

63. May the shit of a thousand camels stain your tent.
—Traditional Arabic curse

64. May the shit of several hundred camels stick to the bottom of your Reeboks.
—Modern Arabic curse

65. Shit-load, a noun 1: a lot of something 2: the contents of one of those trucks that pump out septic tanks

66. Shitting is natural, but not if it's done right.
—Woody Allen, almost

· SHIT HAPPENS ·

67. Dispelling shit myths concerning animals: Raccoons do not make ideal toilet paper. They're rough, and they bite. Squirrels are much better—especially the tail.

68. Like flies on shit, an expression to express delight in something, as flies delight in fresh shit.

69. We shall all shit separately, or we shall all shit together.
    —Early American appeal for unity

70. One bacterium to another: it may be shit to you, but it's home to me.

71. To a Zen Buddhist: one may do well to ponder the sound of shit happening.

·Shit Happens·

72. Shit-shock, a noun, a medical term the sudden rush of feces from the bowels causing the victim to pass out, not known to be fatal under normal conditions.

73. A pile of shit is not harmless merely because no one is consciously offended by it.
—*Our Shit, Ourselves*

74. How to know when you have reached old age: a good shit is more important than a good meal.

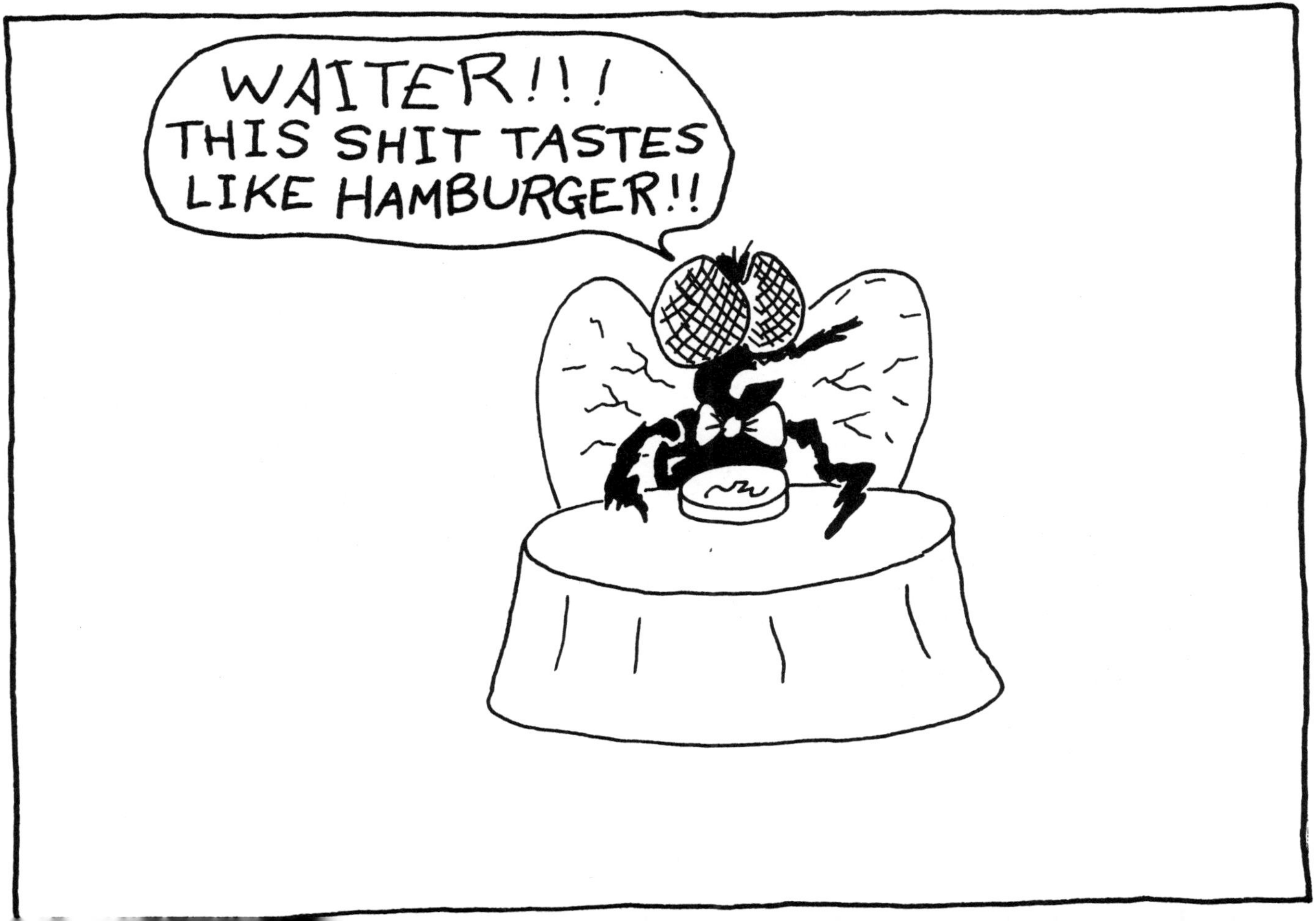
WAITER!!! THIS SHIT TASTES LIKE HAMBURGER!!

· SHIT HAPPENS ·

75. A shitty joke:
Q. What's brown and sits on a piano stool?
A. Beethoven's last movement.

76. If I have to eat one more of these shitty potatoes, I'll puke!
—Attributed to St. Patrick, before his conversion

77. Shit-bag, a noun 1: a disgusting container of shit 2: anyone or anything that meets the requirement of number 1

78. Let your yes be yes, your no be no, and your shit stand on its own.
—The Gospel according to Shit 1:7

79. A shit in the bush is worth two on a toilet.
—*A Naturelover's Guide to Shitting*

· SHIT HAPPENS ·

80. Shit-hole, a noun 1: the place underneath outhouses 2: anyone resembling the place underneath outhouses 3: an anus 4: anyone resembling an anus

81. Not the possession of shit but the effort in struggling to release it brings joy to the shitter.
—*Articles of the Good Shit Club*, Number Nine

82. Don't give me any shit.
—Sign above President Clinton's toilet

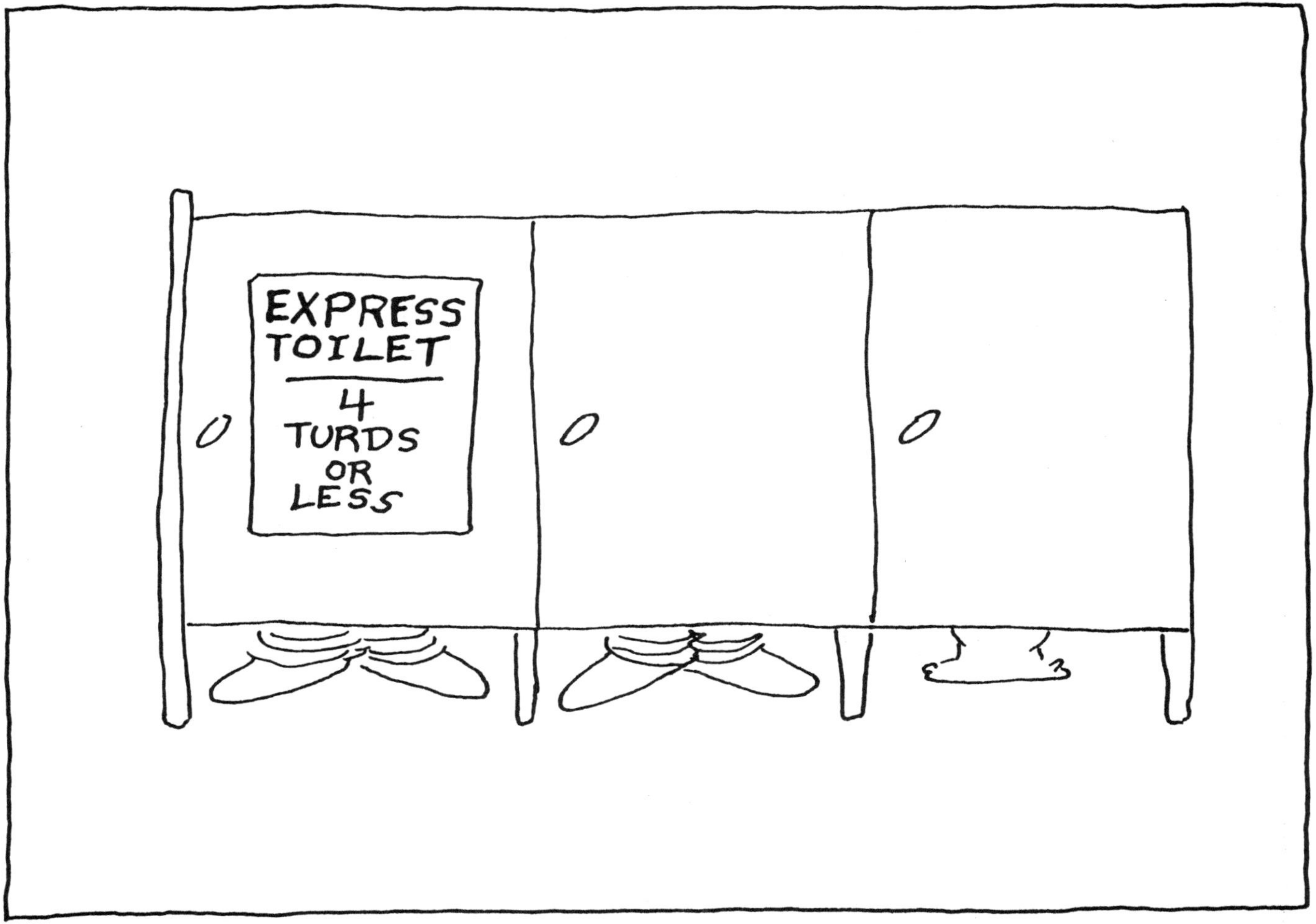
EXPRESS
TOILET
4
TURDS
OR
LESS

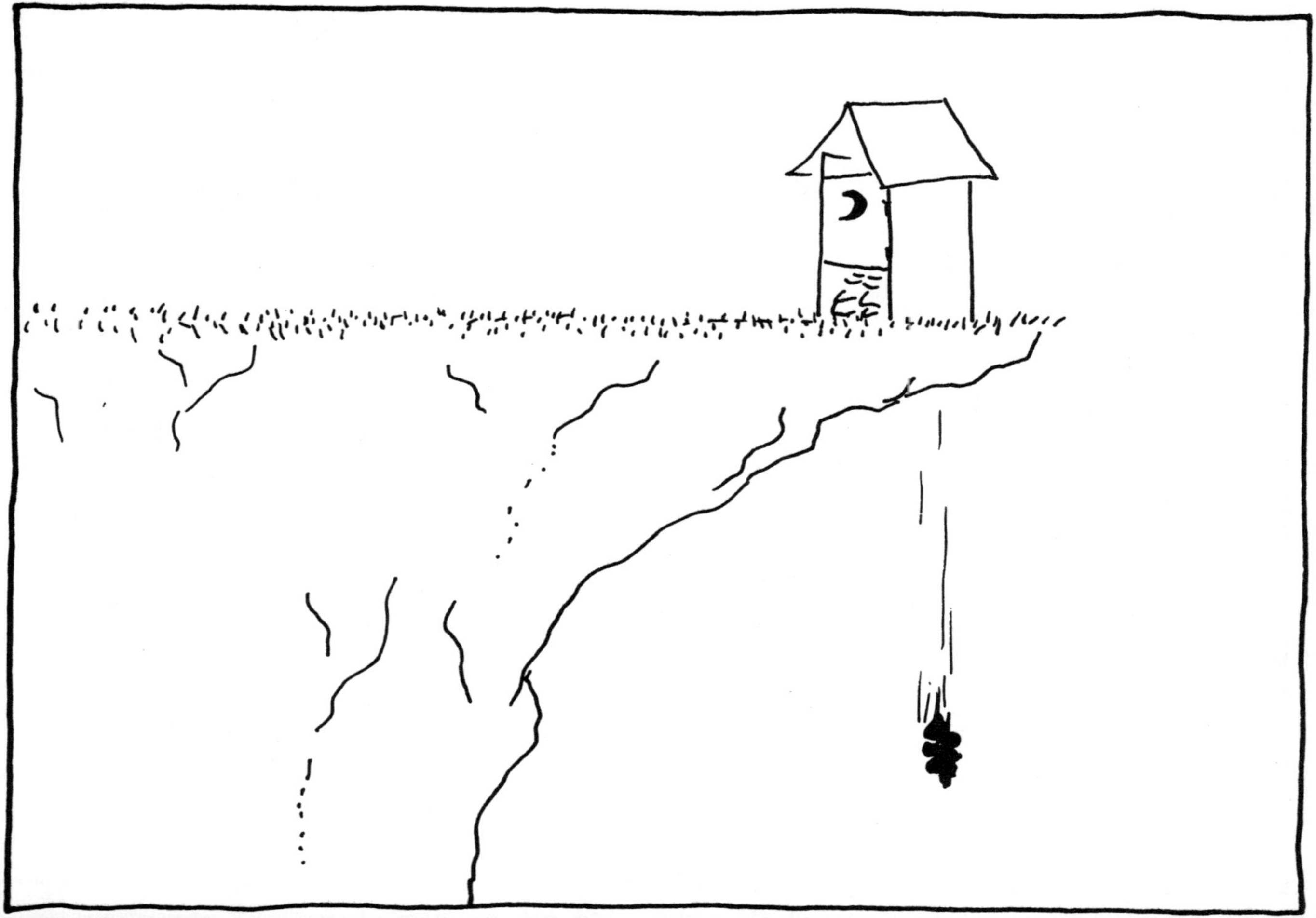

83. Nothing is as inevitable as a piece of shit whose time has come.
    —Szymanski's Surety

84. A good shit is a poor man's best physician.
    —Old Irish Proverb

85. And who's gotta pick up all these donkeyshit-covered palm leaves? Me, that's who!
    —Something the head of the Jerusalem Sanitation Dept. screamed, circa 33 AD

86. Shit out of luck, an expression 1: to have your luck run out 2: to have your shit run out

87. How much happiness is gained, how much sorrow averted, by a frequent and violent shit.
   —Anonymous

88. Q. How can you tell when a lawyer is handing you a line of shit?
   A. His lips are moving.

89. Ordinarily he is insane, but he has lucid moments when he is only full of shit.
   —Close to what Heinrich Heine said about a patient

90. Life is made up of sobs, sniffles, smiles and shit, with shit predominating.
    —*The Better Guide to Babysitting*

91. Any time things appear to be getting less shitty, you have overlooked something.
    —Jack Shit, the "Father of Pessimism," who later changed his name to Smith

92. Holy shit! He's not there? How are we going to explain this?
    —First proclamation of the Divinity of Poo by St. Matt at the last lunch

· SHIT HAPPENS ·

93. Happy as a pig in shit.

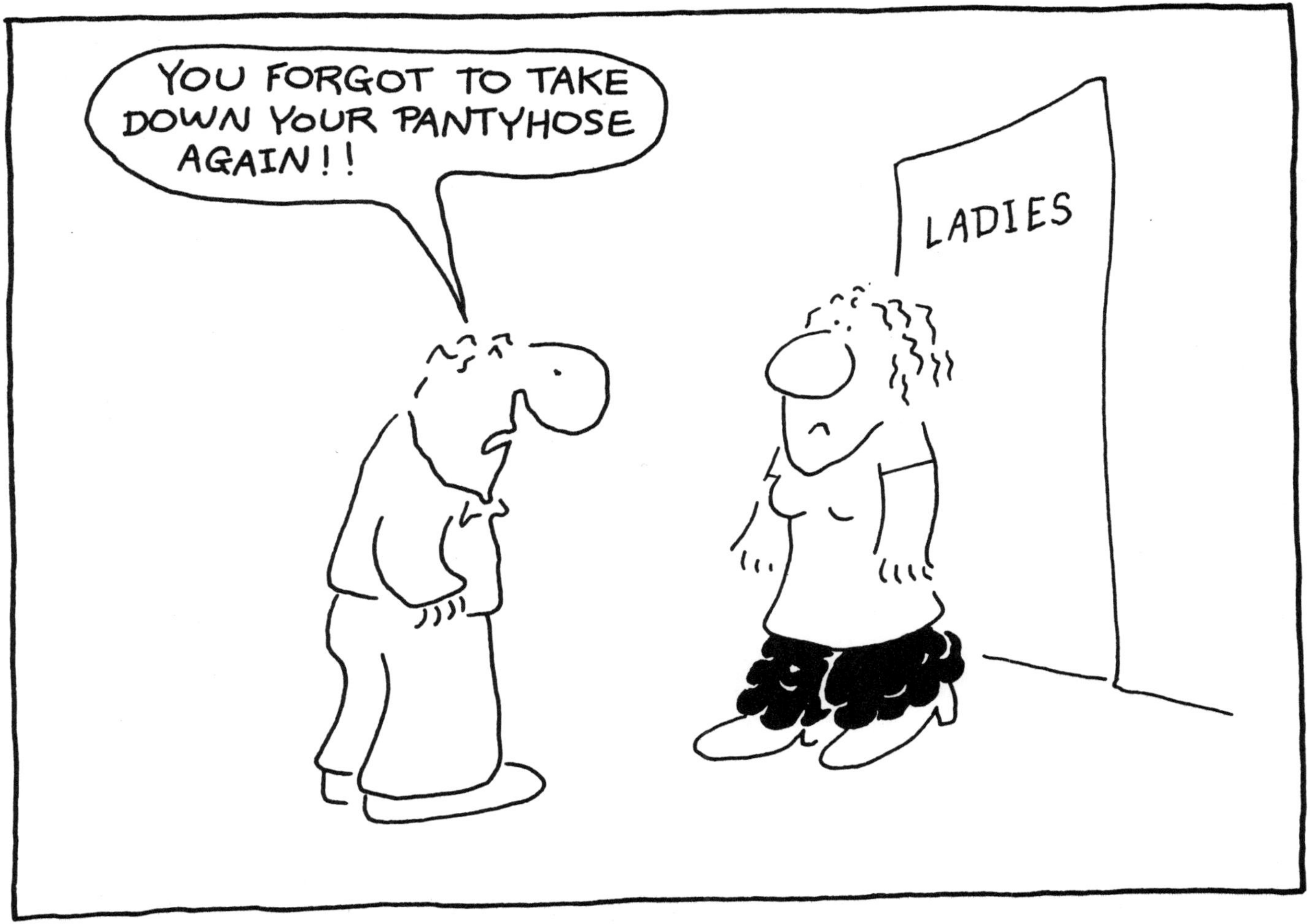
YOU FORGOT TO TAKE DOWN YOUR PANTYHOSE AGAIN!!
LADIES

·SHIT HAPPENS·

94. Shit-head, a noun   sort of like an asshole, but more so

95. How-to book-of-the-month: *Powershitting*, by Dumpmaster Wong Doo.

96. I almost shit my pants, an expression   1: be really scared   2: be really surprised   3: have a really bad case of diarrhea

97. Q. Why does shit stink?
A. Because it's there.
—Overheard at the American Alpine Club, Golden, Colorado

98. It's a good day to shit.
   —Traditional pre-whiteman Sioux greeting

99. Just when you think things can't get any more shitty, someone flushes the toilet.
   —Mac's Law

100. Shit is a slaver in whose holds we are all chained.
   —Attributed to Abraham Lincoln on a bad day

101. Silence is the element in which all great shits are taken.
   —*Articles of the Good Shit Club*, Number Fifteen

· SHIT HAPPENS ·

102. Live long and shit.
    —Less-well-known Vulcan farewell

103. Shit long and prosper.
    —Even lesser-well-known Vulcan farewell

104. One cannot both feast and remain shitless.
    —Old Ashanti Proverb

105. Think shitty, act shitty, be shitty.
    —Motto of the Internal Revenue Service

106. When shit hits the fan, one is left with a messy fan.
    —Modern Chinese Proverb

107. If you realize you're having a nice day, relax. Things will get shitty soon.
—Gray's memo

108. Shitting is the most natural of functions: you can't make it happen, but you can teach people to let it happen.
—Wm. H. Masters, misquoted

109. A shitty poem:
Shits that float
Have made you bloat,
Shits that sink
Will seldom stink.

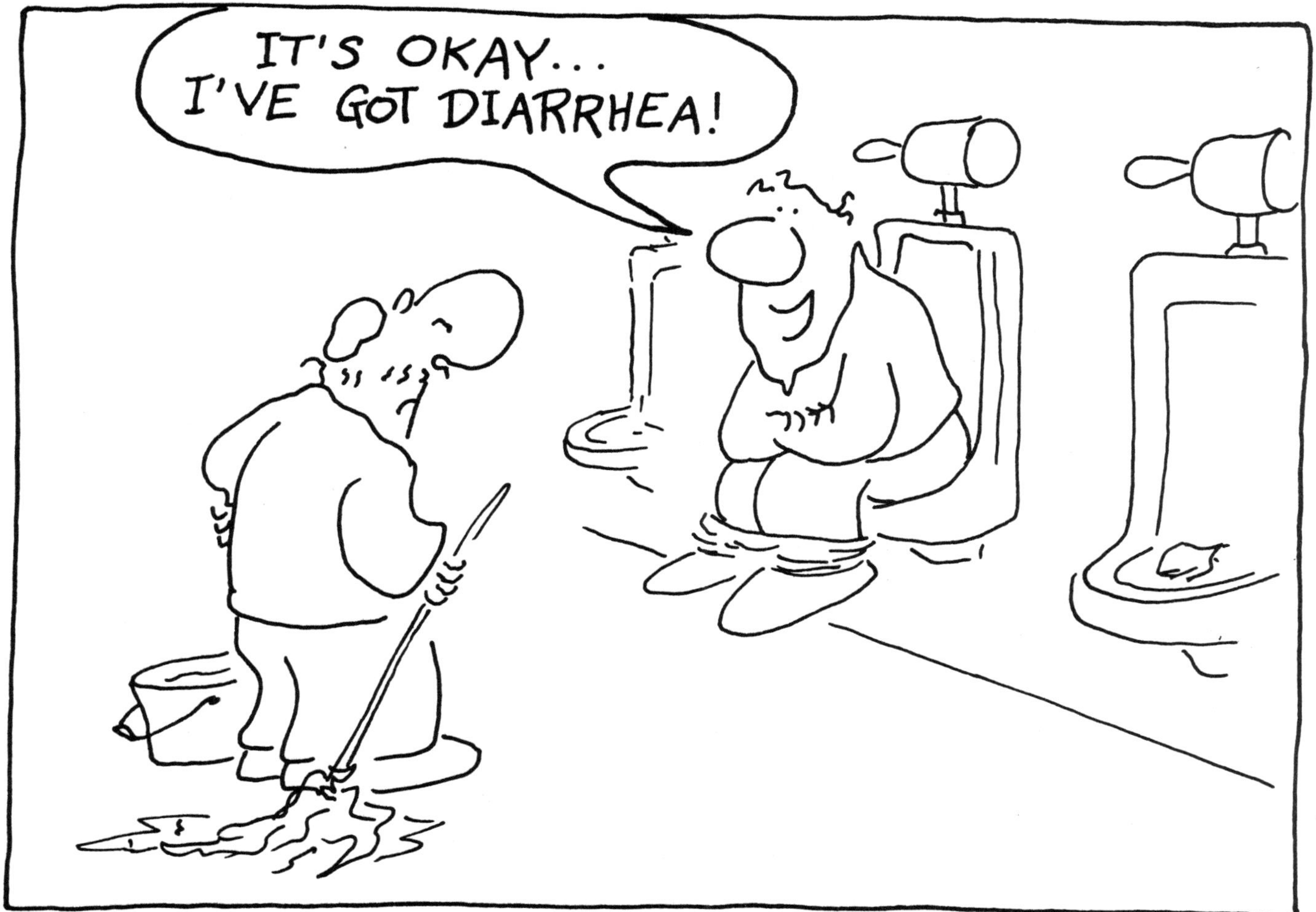
IT'S OKAY...
I'VE GOT DIARRHEA!

SHIT HAPPENS

110. A good shit a day keeps the doctor away.
     —Motto of the Good Shit Club

111. Hi, my name is _____, and I'm a shitoholic.
     —Opening line of every testimonial at meetings of Shitoholics Anonymous

112. To shit or not to shit, that is the question.
     —Motto of Shitoholics Anonymous

113. God grant me the serenity to enjoy good shits, strength to accept bad shits, and the wisdom to know the difference.
     —Prayer of Shitoholics Anonymous

114. To err is human, but a good shit is divine.
    —*Articles of the Good Shit Club*, Number Twenty-nine

115. Eat less, shit more.
    —Uncle Bob's Guaranteed Weight-loss Plan (or your money back)

116. Smile! Tomorrow will be shittier than today.
    —First Principle of Shitty Optimism

117. Let your shit fall where it may.
    —Motto of the Anti-toilet Association

I'M SORRY BUT ALL THE POSITIONS FOR "ASSKISSERS" HAVE BEEN FILLED.
PERSONNEL

118. No matter how shitty something is, somebody will like it.
　　—Principle One, National Society of Manufacturers

119. No matter how shitty something is, somebody will buy it.
　　—Principle Two: National Society of Manufacturers

120. Most things get shittier and shittier.
　　—Law of Entropy restated

121. Mayday, a noun, a call for help 1: shit has hit the fan 2: you're in deep shit 3: shit has happened

·SHIT HAPPENS·

122. Never step in your own shit.
    —Jorian's rule

123. Nothing is ever so shitty that it can't get shittier.
    —Second Principle of Shitty Optimism

124. When the going gets shitty, the intelligent change directions.
    —Lickert's First Lesson

125. Ten pounds of shit in a five-pound bag, an expression 1: something or someone under a lot of pressure 2: on the verge of exploding 3: a bad way to carry shit

· SHIT HAPPENS ·

126. The seat of the shitter is a delightful hiding place for the weary.
 —Thomas Fullofit

· SHIT HAPPENS ·

127. For every shit, there is an equal and opposite re-shit.
    —Simpson's First Law of Shitdynamics

128. Expect a shitty day, and you'll never be disappointed.
    —Third Principle of Shitty Optimism

129. There's no limit to how shitty things can get.
    —Overhead in a White House restroom

130. A flying piece of shit lands on the nearest face.
    —Simpson's Second Law of Shitdynamics

131. Inside every one of us is some shit waiting to come out.

132. To a Protestant: shit happens if you don't work hard enough.

133. If all you have is shit, there's never a good place to put it.
    —First Dictum of Pessimism

134. If all you have is shit, there's always a good place to put it.
    —First Dictum of Optimism

135. Shit never comes out the way you thought it would.
    —Bernouli's observation

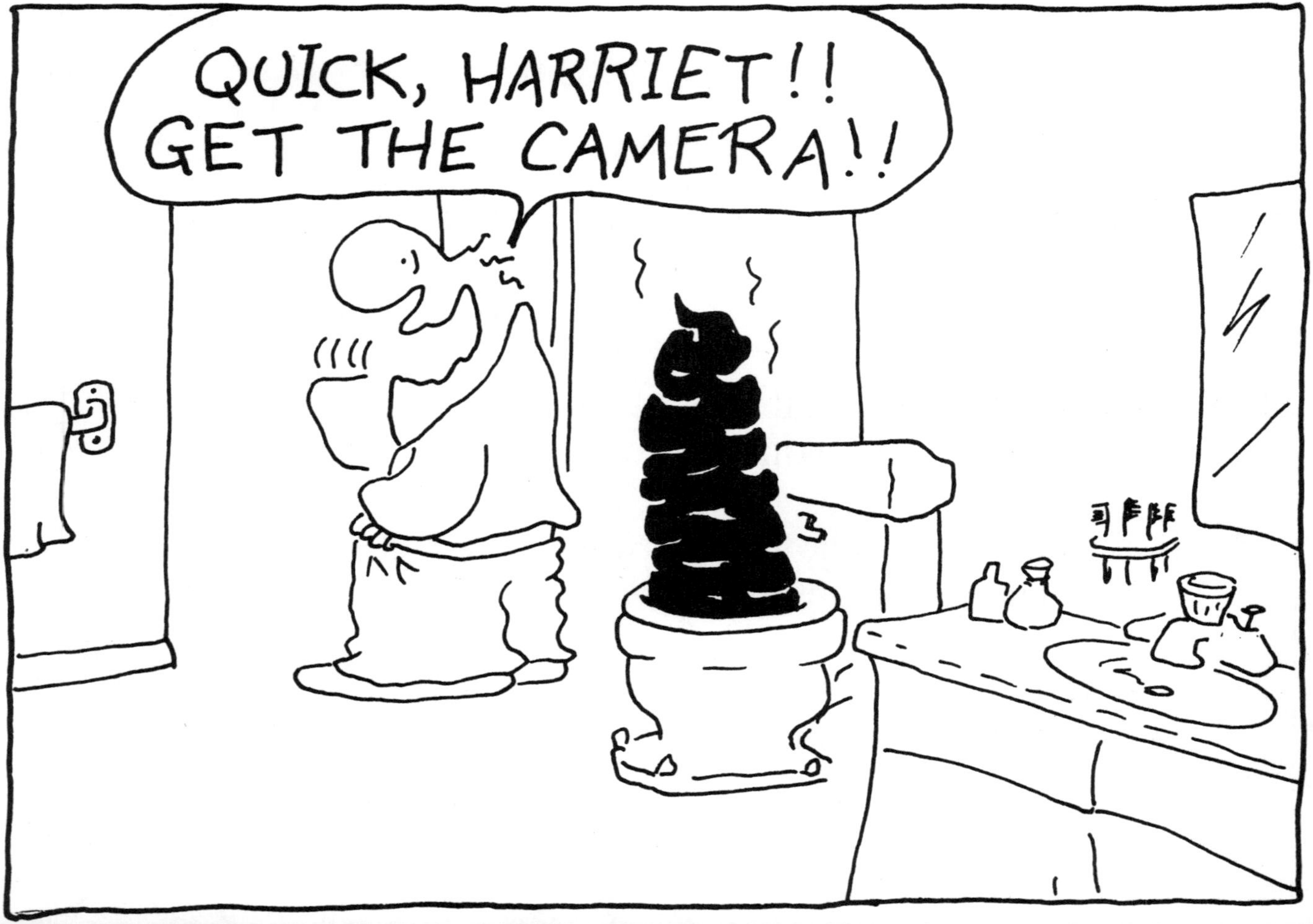
QUICK, HARRIET!! GET THE CAMERA!!

· SHIT HAPPENS ·

136. Shyness in taking a shit is perhaps the greatest characteristic distinguishing man from other animals.

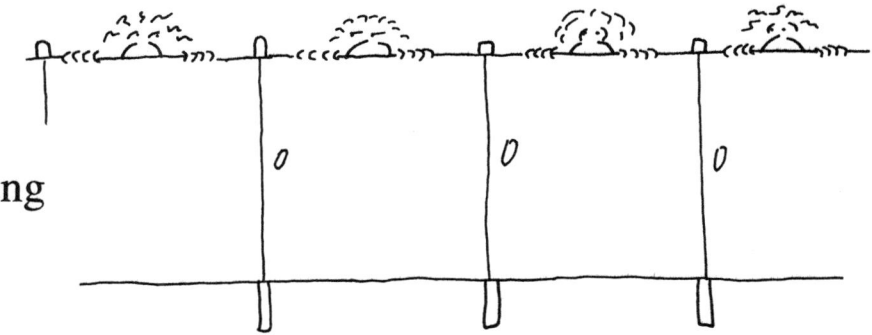

Shit Happens

137. Just because it works doesn't mean it's not a piece of shit.
 —Peter's Precept

138. Just because it's a piece of shit doesn't mean it won't work.
 —Corollary to Peter's Precept

139. It is easier to step in shit than to pick it up.
 —Peter's Wife's Precept

140. It is easier to pick up shit before you step in it.
 —Corollary to Peter's Wife's Precept

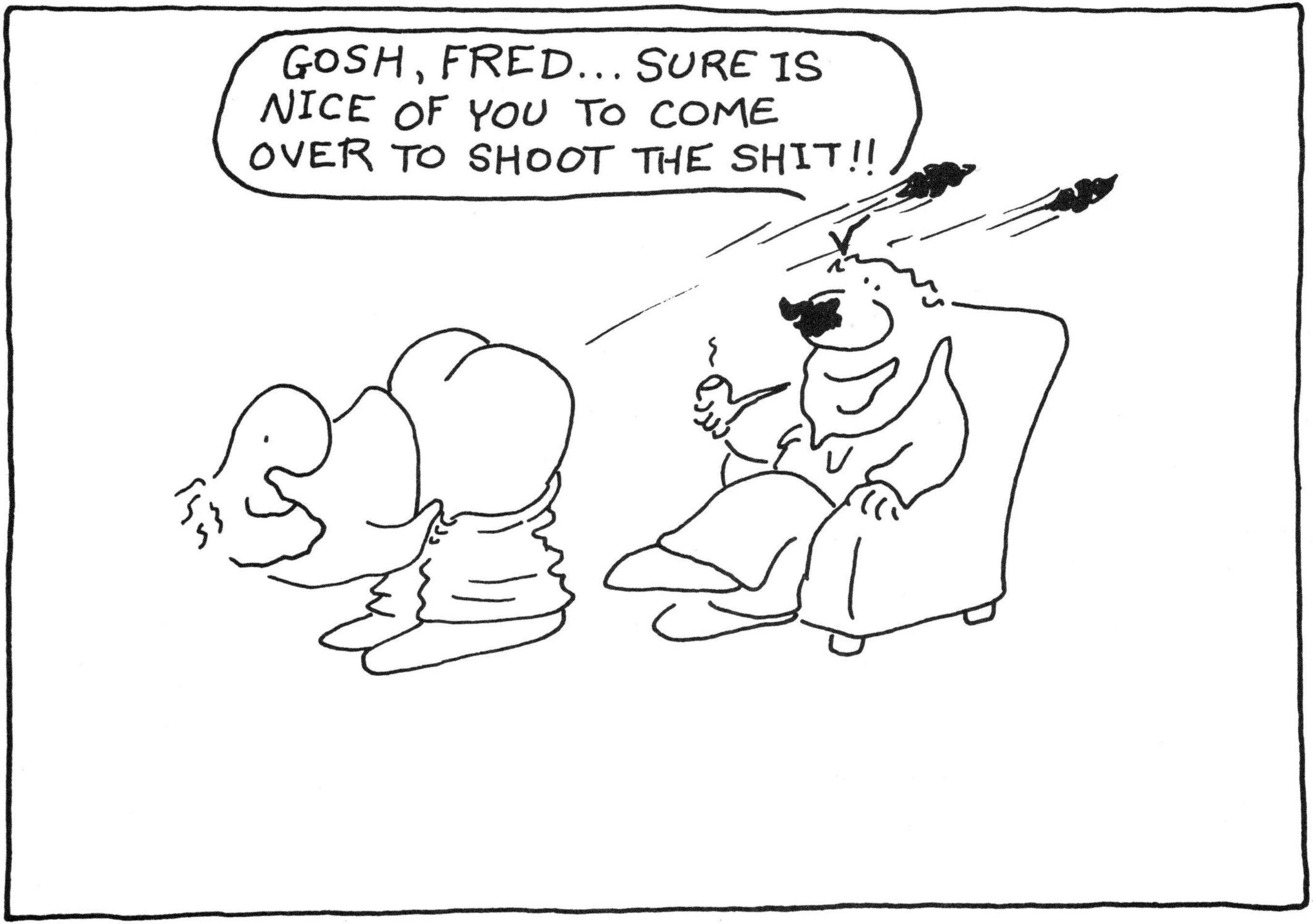
GOSH, FRED... SURE IS NICE OF YOU TO COME OVER TO SHOOT THE SHIT!!

· SHIT HAPPENS ·

141. A hearty laugh and a good shit are the best cures.
—Old Irish Proverb

142. Never sit down on the toilet before checking the toilet paper dispenser.
    —Musgrove's Law of Shitting

143. A shitty thought: if you are what you eat, what do you leave in the toilet?

144. Someone who smiles when things turn out shitty knows someone else he or she can blame it on.
    —Lickert's Fourth Lesson

145. In defaex veritas.
    —Old Latin Proverb ("In Shit Lies Truth")

· SHIT HAPPENS ·

146. Thou shalt not covet thy neighbor's shit.
    —The Eleventh Commandment

147. When it is not necessary to take a shit, it is necessary to not take a shit.
    —From Ms. Manner's *Rules of Shittyquette*

148. If you can't dazzle someone with your brilliance, baffle them with your bullshit.

149. In every load of bullshit, there is an element of truth.
    —Bubba's axiom

150. In every load of truth, there is an element of bullshit.
 —Corollary to Bubba's axiom

151. A wise man and his shit are soon parted.

152. Where you shit depends on where you sit.
 —Epstein's Law

153. Of this does wisdom consist: knowing when to let shit lay.
 —Buckman's Principle

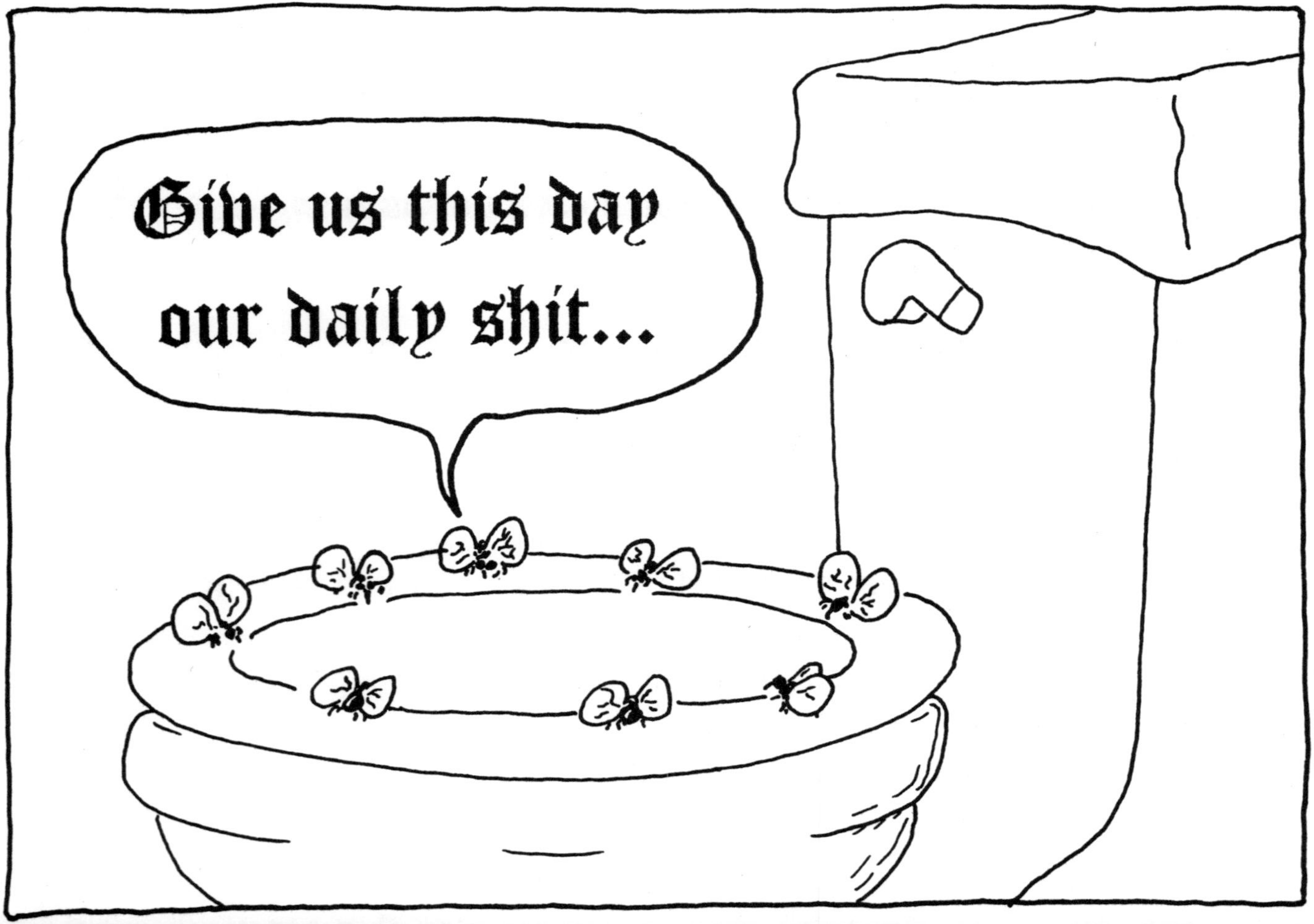
Give us this day our daily shit...

154. Any shitty opinion can be supported by consulting enough experts.

155. Hot shit, a noun 1: something made well 2: something done well 3: someone who thinks they're made well or they've done well

156. Everyone is full of shit at one time or another.
     —Jim's pearl

157. Never trust anyone who stands to lose less than you do if everything goes to shit.
     —Lickert's Fifth Lesson

Shit Happens

158. The chance that something shitty will happen is the direct inverse of how much you don't want it to happen.
—Dr. Rose's Reverse Probability Law

159. One who says he flushes without looking will probably tell other lies as well.
—Hubbell's Shit Theorem

160. A good shit is one in which you can finish the entire article and no one knocks on the door.
—Spike's definition

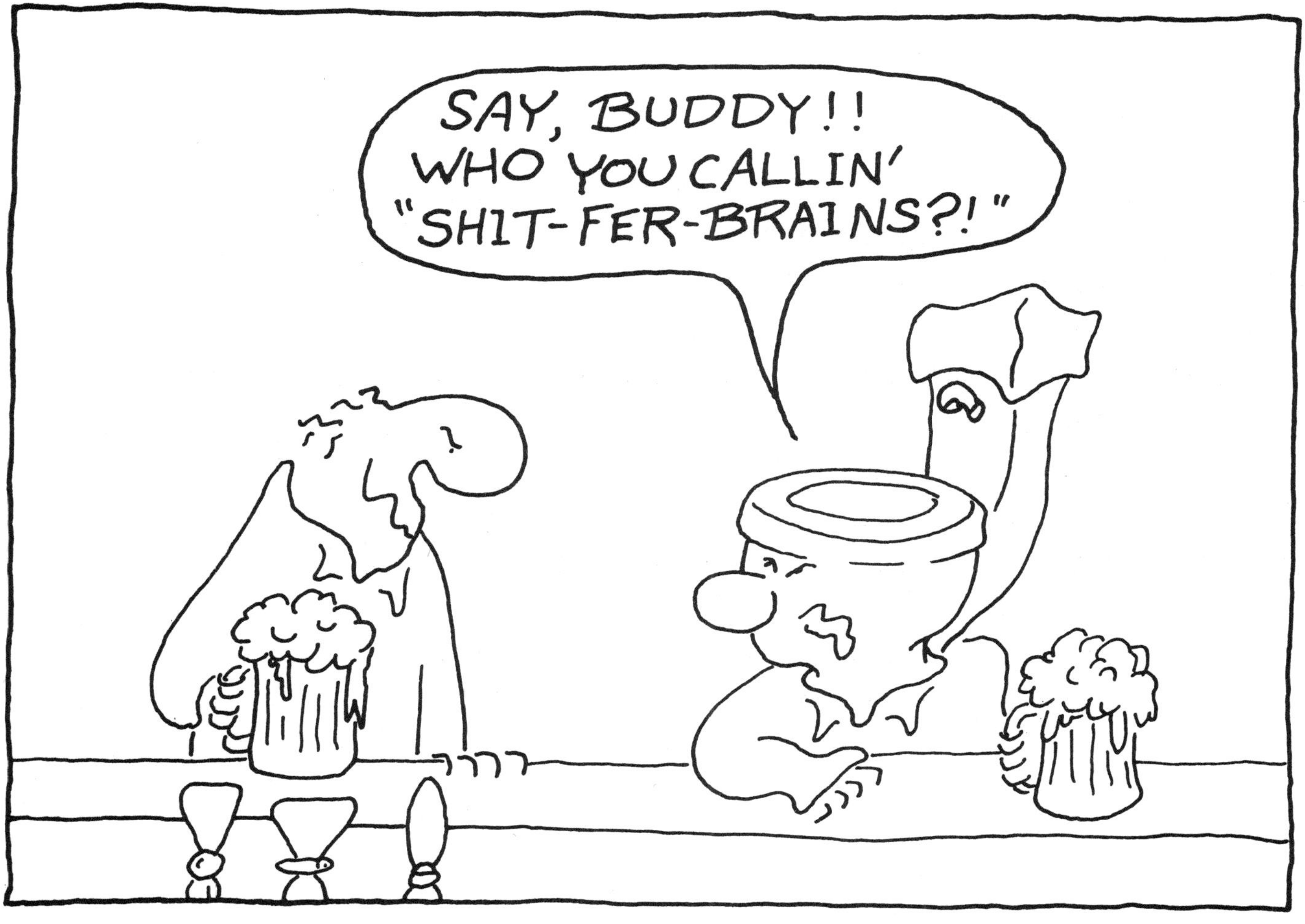
SAY, BUDDY!!
WHO YOU CALLIN'
"SHIT-FER-BRAINS?!"

·Shit Happens·

161. When words fail, excuse yourself to take a shit.
     —Spikes's solution

162. The time required to take a shit is not subtracted from your life's total sum.
     —Frank's fallacy

163. For a Seventh Day Adventist: shit happens on Saturdays.

164. Shit is easier to get into than to get out of.
     —De Kay's Constant

165. Jack shit, an expression 1: something of little or no value
2: a name you'd really hate to be stuck with

166. The superior shit is enjoyed. The mediocre shit is attended to. The inferior shit is rushed.
—Ancient Chinese wisdom

167. To a scatologist, a shitty day is a good day.

168. Seashitless, a noun, a medical term 1: being unable to take a dump on a boat caused by excessive motion of the boat
2: known to be fatal on really long sea voyages

·SHIT HAPPENS·

169. No man knoweth from whence the wind blows . . . unless it blows from the shithouse.
    —The Gospel According to Shit 2:23

170. Just because it don't stink don't mean it ain't shit.
    —Motto of the Chicago Shitters Association

171. Nature is that lady who calls us to take a shit even when the weather is most unappealing.
    —*A Naturelover's Guide to Shitting*

· SHIT HAPPENS ·

172. Shed your clothes completely, and at the stroke of midnight beneath a cloudless moon, walk three times around a house throwing a handful of toilet paper over your shoulder with each step. If no one sees you, you will soon take a shit.
—Old Dutch cure for constipation

173. There is no evidence correlating the quality of a fart with the quality of a shit.
 —*New England Journal of Shitology*, 11:17:93

174. Those who can, shit; those who can't, wish they could.
 —One of life's few truths

175. Never do today any shit-work that can be put off until tomorrow.
 —Root's Rule

176. When shit hits the fan, it will be distributed unevenly.
 —Fig's First Law of Shit Dispersal

177. When shit hits the fan, the safest place to be is in another building.
—Fig's Constant

178. Shit-faced, an adjective 1: intoxicated 2: describing one near the fan when shit hits it

179. Once the shit's out of the bag, you can never get it back in the same bag.
—Carey's Conundrum

· SHIT HAPPENS ·

180. It is difficult to smell like a rose when you're standing in shit.
     —Old Latvian Proverb

181. If you ever really need to take a shit in an airport, your plane will be on time.
     —Bennett's Dilemma

182. If at first you don't succeed, take a laxative.
     —*Articles of the Good Shit Club,* Addendum One

183. If you end up with shit on your face, act like it was intentional.
     —Lickert's sixth lesson

TWO ALL SHIT PATTIES, SPECIAL SAUCE, LETTUCE, CHEESE, PICKLES, ONIONS, ON A SESAME SEED BUN!

SHIT HAPPENS

184. Your need to shit is inversely proportional to the availability of a place to shit.
—Second Dictum of Pessimism

185. Give me liberty, and don't give me no shit!
—Battle Cry of the First Georgia Rifles, 1776

186. Your need to shit in a car will grow in direct proportion to the lack of places to shit along the road.
—Third Dictum of Pessimism

187. The act of shitting should be noble and pleasant, but it is often filled with labor and anxiety.
    —*Practical Proctology*

188. If you cannot obtain shit from begging, at least learn when to stop.
    —Old Hindu Proverb

189. I will lift up mine eyes unto the pills from whence cometh my shit when constipated.
    —The Gospel According to Shit 3:30

· SHIT HAPPENS ·

190. There's never any paper left on the roll when you take a dump at a friend's house.
—Corollary to Murphy's Shit Law

191. The probability of having to take a shit increases when you are with someone you don't want to excuse yourself from.

192. If you don't care whether or not you can take a good shit, you've never been constipated.
    —Carey's Constant

193. To a Catholic: if shit happens, feel guilty and ask forgiveness.

194. Good times come and good times go, but bad shit accumulates.
    —Roger's Observation

195. People can be divided into two groups—the shitty and the non-shitty—and the shitty do the dividing.
    —Peter's Postulate

196. The most exciting part of any movie takes place when you've had to rush out to take a shit.
    —Fourth Dictum of Pessimism

197. Built like a brick shithouse, an expression 1: well-made 2: well-proportioned 3: made of rectangular blocks that smell bad

198. Good shitters never die; they are just wiped out at the end.

199. No matter where you go, you'll have to take a shit.
    —First Indisputable Shit Law

200. Anticipation of taking a shit is never as good as the real thing.
    —Second Indisputable Shit Law

201. International shit guideline: never eat within two days of getting on a South American bus.

202. No matter how shitty a dessert tastes, someone will eat it.
    —The Kitchen Constant

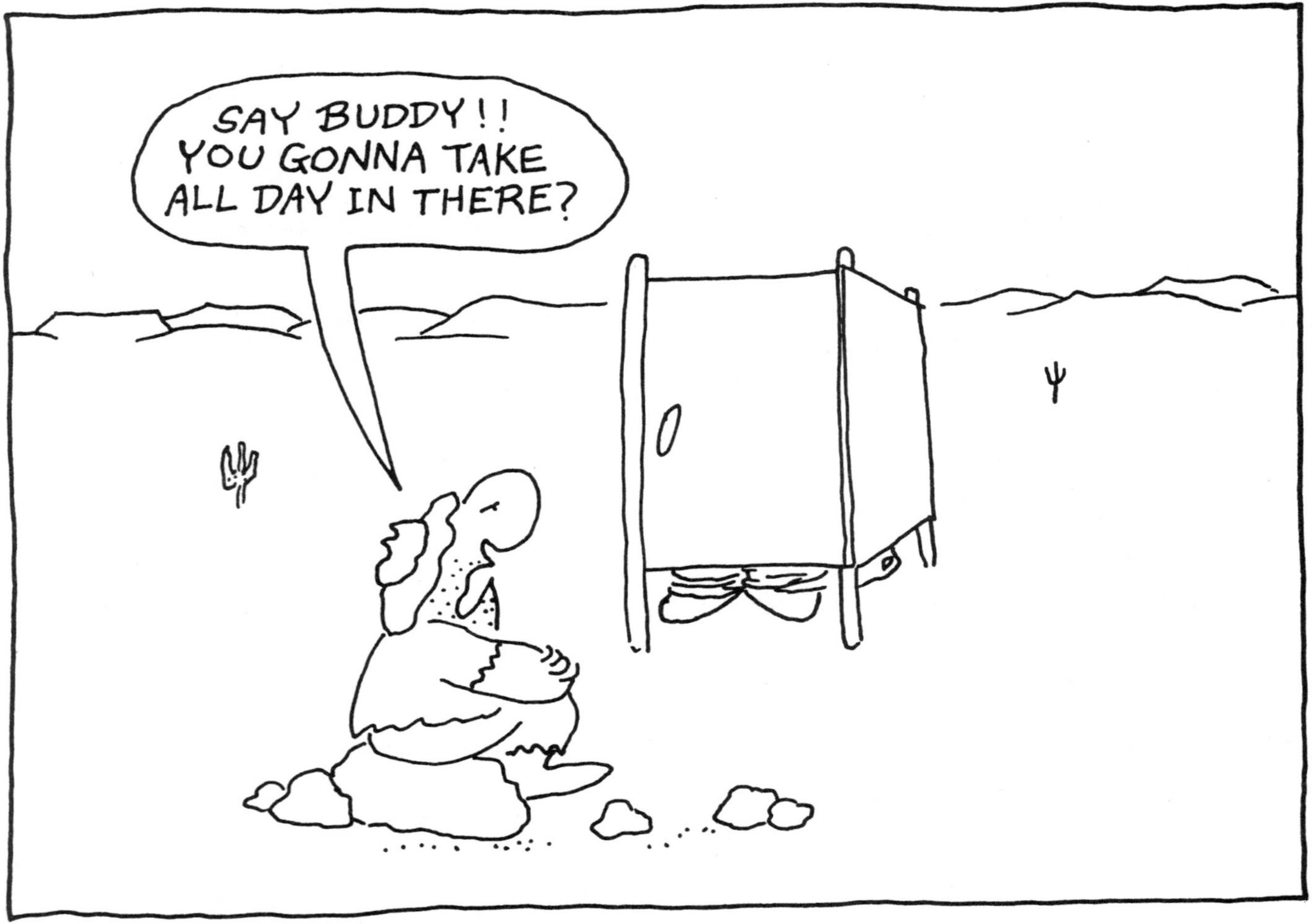
SAY BUDDY!! YOU GONNA TAKE ALL DAY IN THERE?

203. The smelliest shits are the ones most likely to plug the toilet.
　　—Polly's Postulate

204. The length of a minute is determined by how bad you have to take a shit.
　　—Law of One-toilet Homes

205. When you are most relaxed on the shitter, the phone will ring.
　　—Tarter's Tantrum

206. One size fits all.
　　—The Porcelain Shitter Manufacturers' Guarantee

· SHIT HAPPENS ·

207. The well-trodden path leads to the shithouse.
　　　—Old Southern Proverb

208. No matter how good you get at it, you'll always have to shit again.

209. It is always easier to take a shit than to give a shit.
　　　—Amber's Axiom

210. It is always easier to give shit than to take shit.
　　　—Amber's Addendum

211. Advice from the Old West: never kick a pile of shit on a hot day.

212. Advice from the new West: Never kick a pile of shit with new boots.

213. Shitting is at least as much art as it is science.
    —*Practical Proctology*

214. No matter how much you pay for your toilet, your shit smells the same.
    —The Bathroom Constant

Shit Happens

215. Eat shit, an expression 1: an angry and graphic comeback, like "drop dead" 2: an unpleasant meal

216. It is better to slip on a pile of shit than to fall to the bottom of the outhouse.
    —Old wive's tale

217. It be better to fall to the bottom of the outhouse than to be flushed down the toilet.
    —New wive's tale

DAMMIT, FRED!!! WHEN ARE YOU GONNA FIX THE LEAK IN YOUR COLOSTOMY BAG??!!

218. There are two times you should spare no expense: choosing your doctor and decorating your bathroom.
    —*Articles of the Good Shit Club,* Number Thirty-one

219. Closing your bathroom door should assure you at least fifteen minutes of undisturbed privacy.
    —*Articles of the Good Shit Club,* Number Thirty-two

220. Klingon, a noun 1: a little piece of shit that sticks to the hairs around Uranus

221. The person who knows everything has much to learn, but the person who don't know shit just don't know shit.

222. No one can think clearly when they have to take a shit.
    —*Doo-doo and Mind*

223. If you want a good place to shit, prepare to spend some time looking for it.
    —*A Naturelover's Guide to Shitting*

224. To a Moslem: if shit happens, take a hostage.

225. Experience teaches you to recognize a good shit when you've taken one.
    —John Doowey

· SHIT HAPPENS ·

226. When in doubt, take a shit.
—Malcom Feces

227. A shitty thought: nothing is impossible except to the constipated.

228. If you can't laugh at yourself when you have to take a shit, make fun of someone else who has to take a shit.

229. A wise man is known for the shit he avoids.
—Ancient Japanese Proverb

· SHIT HAPPENS ·

230. Someone who doesn't know shit from shinola is not able to distinguish between a pile of doo-doo and brown, shiny shoe polish.

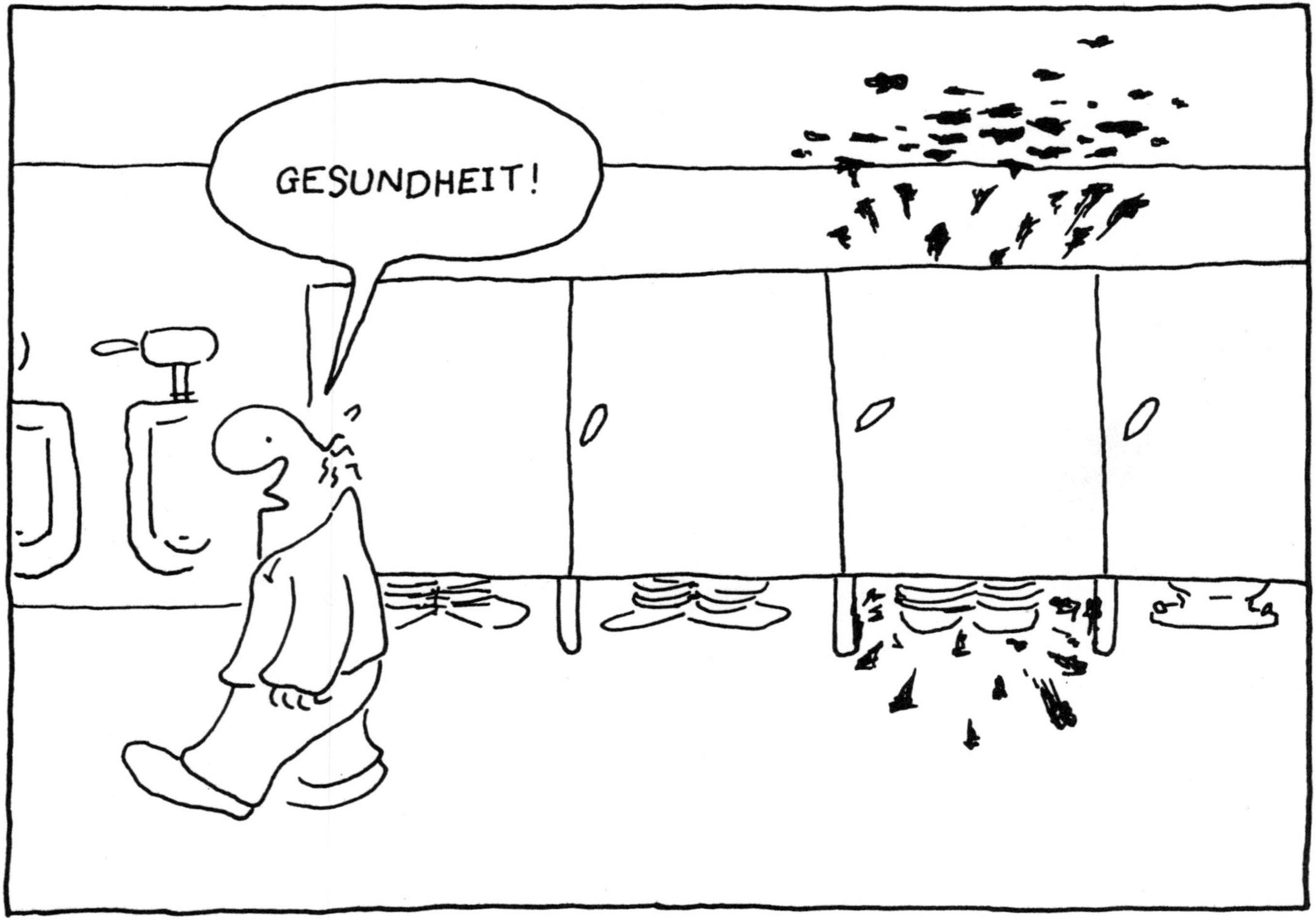
GESUNDHEIT!

231. It is easier to hold your tongue than to hold your shit.
 —Ancient New York Proverb

232. Shit is cheap. All white men are full of it.
 —Cheyenne Chief Two-toilets

233. You can't save time and you can't save shit. Both decompose regardless.

234. A really bad shit is the revenge of really good food.
 —*A Fat Lover's Guide to Eating*

·SHIT HAPPENS·

235. One of the surest signs of an approaching nervous breakdown is belief in your own shit.
—Bertrand Russell, almost

236. Know your own shit.
—Socratease

237. When attending the school of hard shits, it is better to remain regular.
—Attributed to Kung Fu-poo

238. It is better to slip in shit and regain your balance than to fall on your face.

239. To love your shit is the beginning of a lifelong romance.
—*Articles of the Good Shit Club,* Number Forty-nine

240. He who shits, lasts.
—Merry Cess Poole

241. The need to shit divides people into two types: those who relax and enjoy it, and those who don't.
—Joanne's Distinction

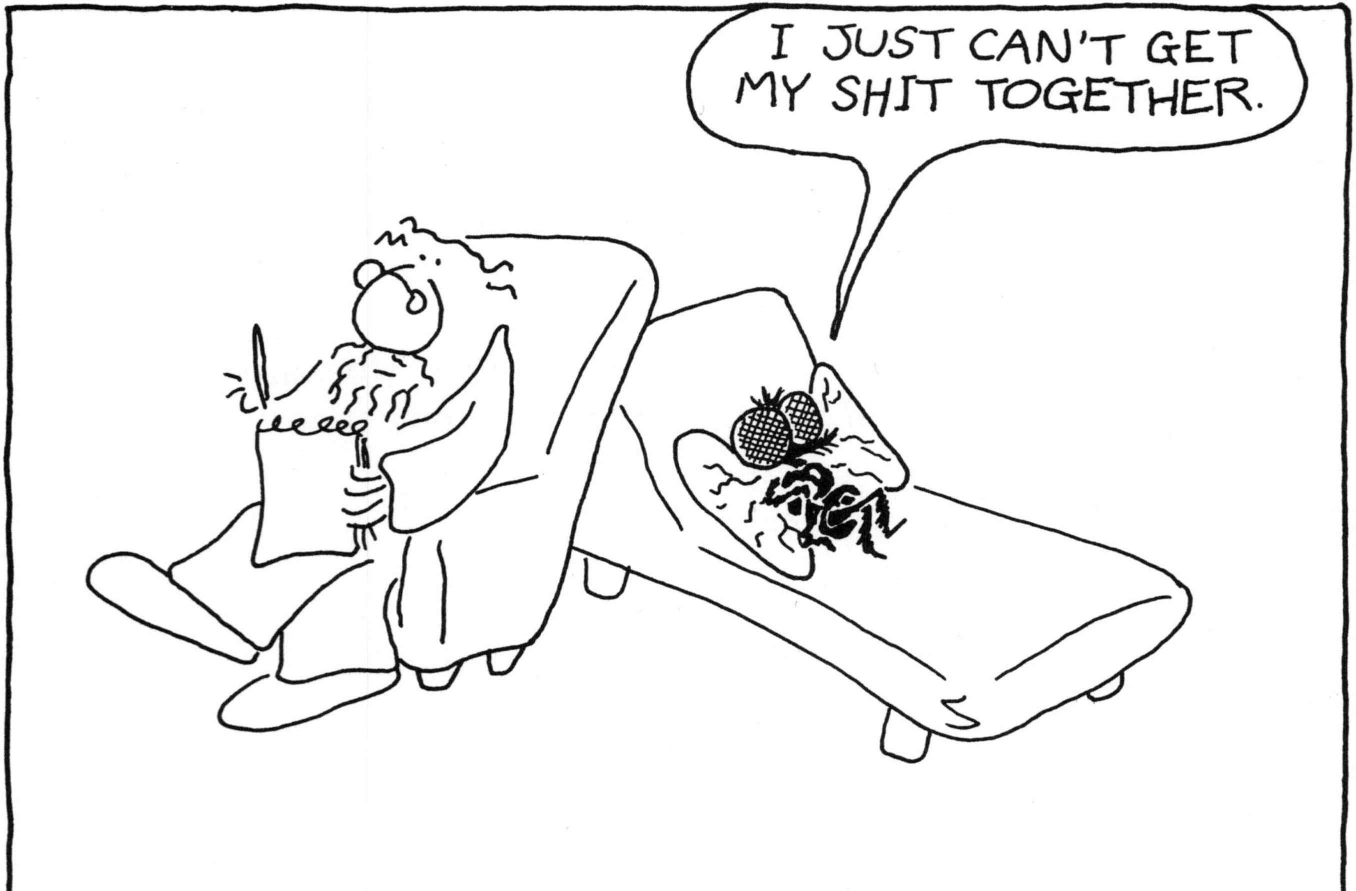
I JUST CAN'T GET MY SHIT TOGETHER.

242. Shit is what happens when you're making other plans.
   —With apologies to John Lennon

243. There is more to life than shitting. But it'll have to wait.
   —*Everything I Know I Learned in the Bathroom*

244. If you learn to love taking a shit, you'll never have a bad day.
   —*Articles of the Good Shit Club,* Number Forty-two

245. There is no task so shitty that it can't be made shittier.
   —Fifth Dictum of Pessimism

246. Stand up to be counted, but sit down to shit.
    —*Secrets of a Happy Life*

247. It's not over till the paperwork is done.
    —*How to Shit Well*

248. Shit deals gently only with those who take it gently.
    —Anatole France, misquoted to say

249. All the world's an outhouse, and all the men and women merely shitters.
—Shakespeare, an early attempt

250. Shit is, above all, a gift you give to yourself.
—*Articles of the Good Shit Club,* Number Fifty-two

251. Shit is the gift that keeps on giving.
—*Smells I Have Known and Loved*

252. Express a shitty opinion of yourself occasionally. It'll prove to your friends you know how to tell the truth.
—Ed Howe, nearly

253. The art of being wise is recognizing shit for what it is.
—William James' brother

254. Always be willing to call shit shit when you hear it. But leave the room immediately after.

255. To a Jew: shit always happens to me!

256. Shit never gives, it only lends.
   —Old Swedish Proverb

257. Don't lean over backward so far that you fall in your own shit.

258. Everyone must shit with his own anus.
   —Old English Proverb

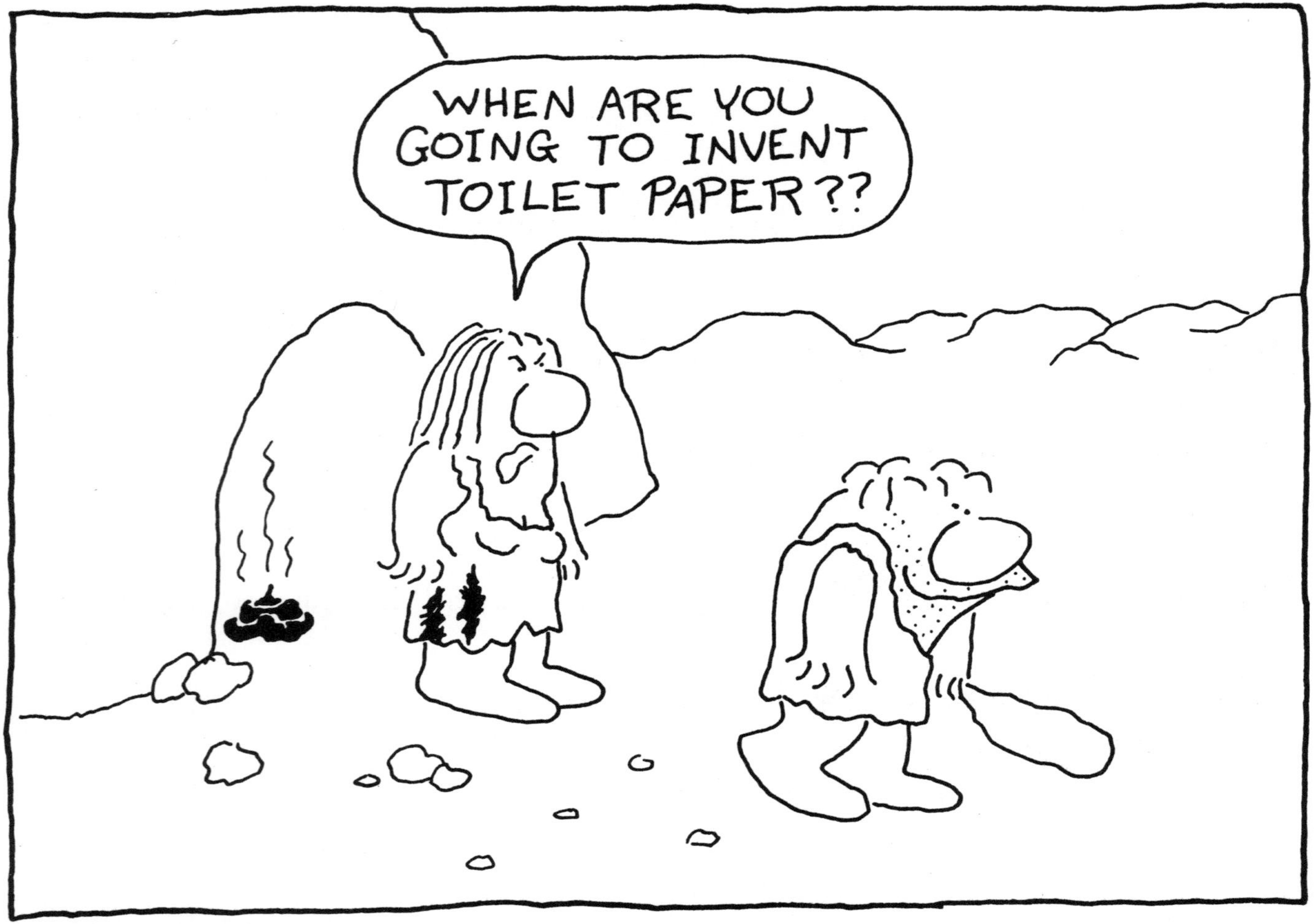
WHEN ARE YOU GOING TO INVENT TOILET PAPER??

259. T'is shit, not strength, that governs a man's bowels.
 —Thomas Fullofit

260. It is easier to appear worthy of shit not our own than of that which is ours.
 —*Maxims* of Rochefoucauld, liberally translated

261. If life must not be taken too seriously, then so neither must shit.
 —Samuel Buttler

262. Life is shit, and all things show it. I thought so once, and now I know it.
 —Almost John Gay's epitaph

263. Man's "progress" is but a gradual discovery that his questions don't mean shit.
 —*The Wisdom of Shit*

264. There is but one step from the sublime to the totally shitty.
 —Attributed to Napoleon

265. It is honorable to be accused of being shitty by those who deserve to be accused of being shitty.
 —Old Latin Proverb

· SHIT HAPPENS ·

266. If you want to shit with the big dogs, use the neighbor's lawn.

267. Who shits too much accomplishes little.
 —Old German Proverb

268. My own view, for what it's worth, is this: shitting is lovely. There cannot be too much of it. It is self-limiting if it is satisfactory, and satisfaction diminishes tension and clears the mind for attention and learning.
 —B. Tilton, MS (Master Of Shitting)

269. It is not enough to aim for the shitter; you must hit it.
 —Old Italian Proverb

270. He who can shit freely is a prince among those who can't.
 —Thomas Fullofit

271. One who takes big shits leaves big traces.
 —Old Burmese Proverb

272. One who takes a big shit after constipation forgets about God.
 —Old Ethiopian Proverb

273. Shitting is one of nature's sweetest gratifications.
 —*On Life and Shit*

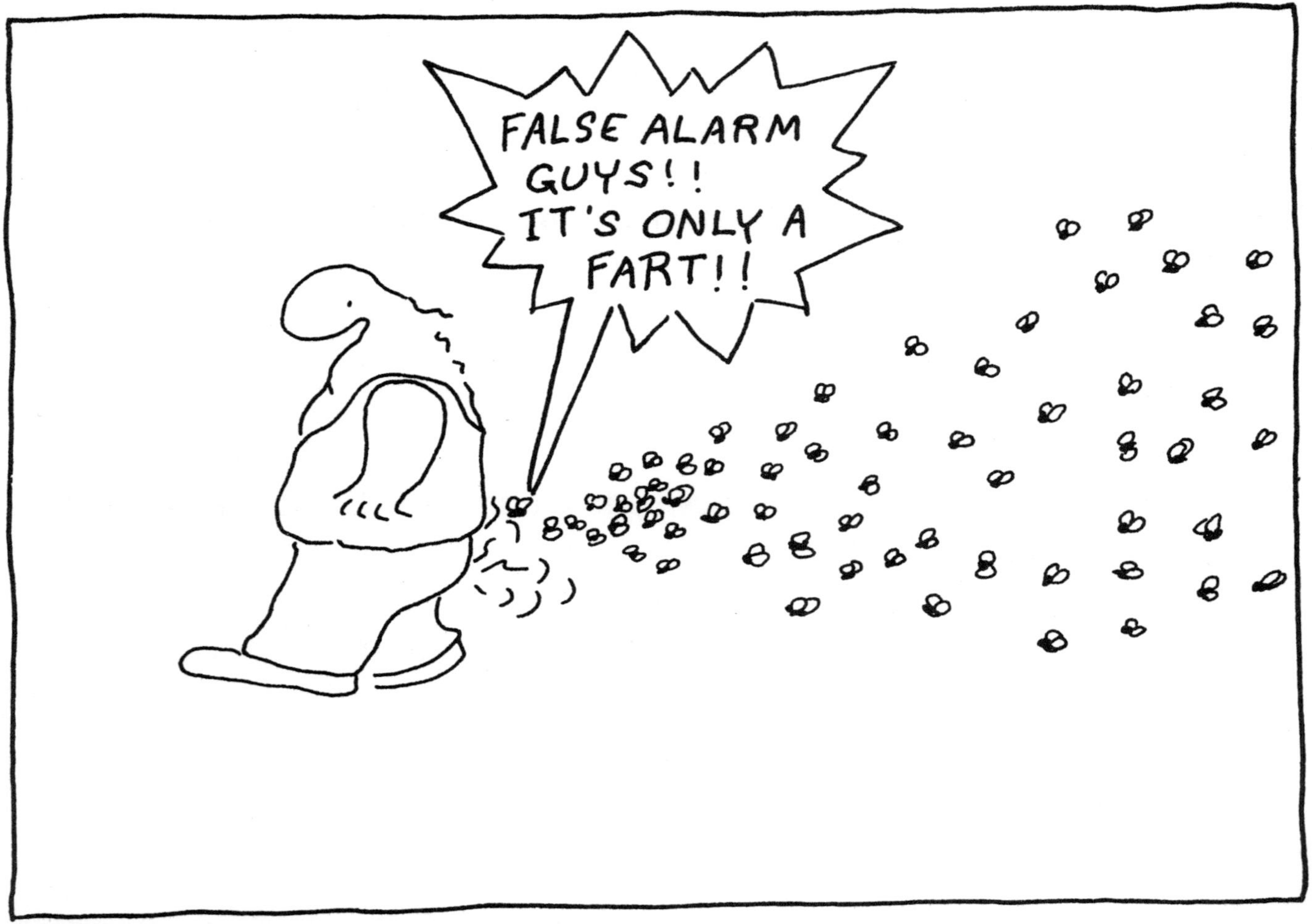
FALSE ALARM GUYS!! IT'S ONLY A FART!!

274. If we cannot shit where we will, we must shit where we can.
   —Old Yiddish Proverb

275. A good shit is itself good medicine.
   —*Practical Proctology*

276. Knowing your shit, an expression 1: to be very knowledgeable in your area of expertise 2: to be a scatologist

277. Burn not your house to drive away the stink of shit.
   —Thomas Fullofit

278. A shitless man is like an axe on an embroidery frame.
   —Old Malay Proverb

279. The shithouse is a cynic. It tells all.
   —Victor Hugego

280. A good shit can only be compared with music and with prayer.
   —*On Life and Shit*

281. The more shit we have, the less satisfied we are with it.

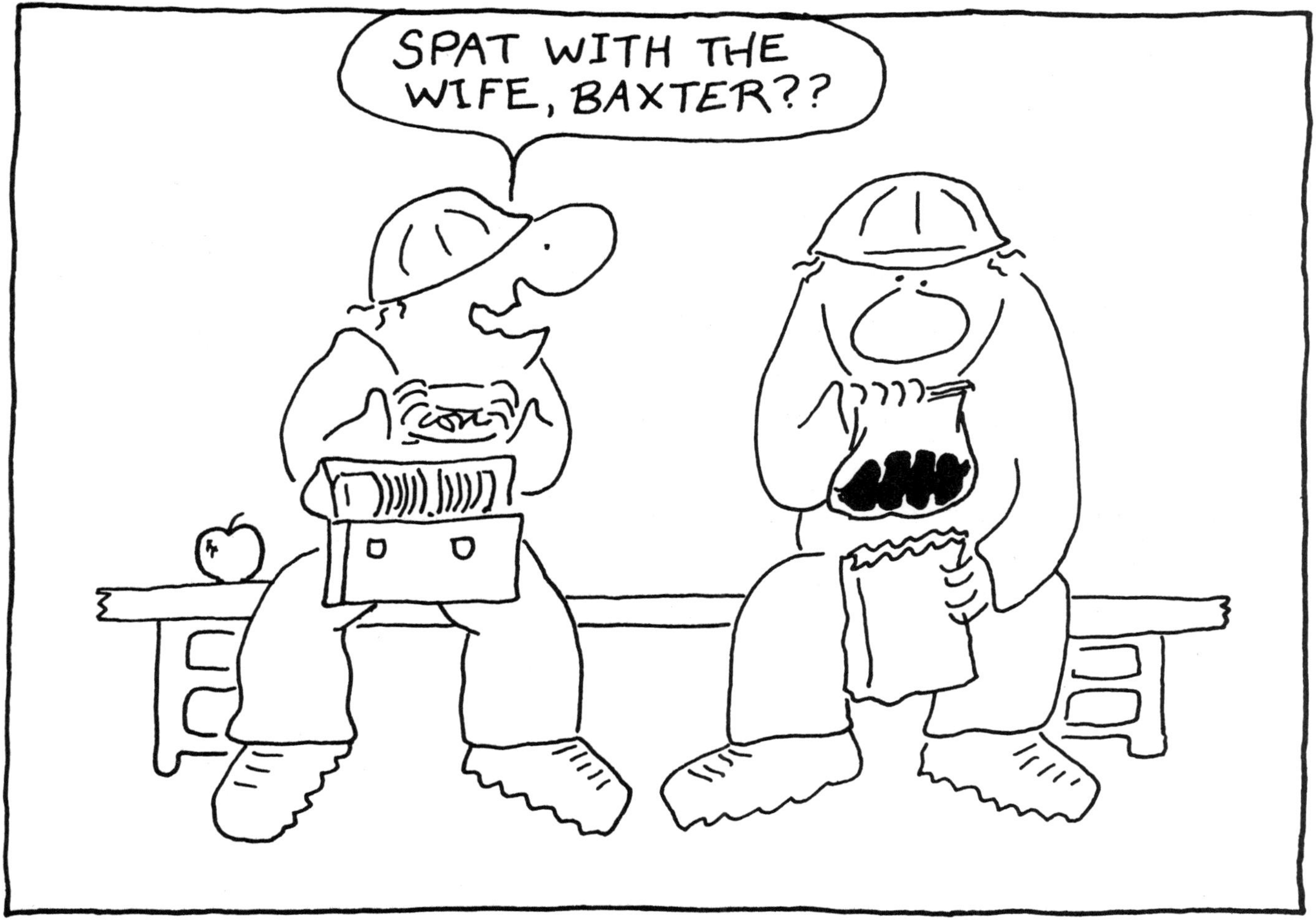
SPAT WITH THE WIFE, BAXTER??

· SHIT HAPPENS ·

282. He stalked the night, as silent as a ghost, and carried away, never to be seen again, all the children that had shit their pants.
—*Tales of the Terrible Shitman*

283. Good shit is good only because bad shit is in such large supply.

284. Outside the snow is falling, and friends are calling, eat shit! eat shit! eat shit!
—*When Christmas songwriters go bad*

· SHIT HAPPENS ·

285. No shit, Sherlock.
—Watson to Holmes, after another irritating display of elementary logic

SHIT HAPPENS

286. You never outgrow your need to shit.
    —*The Child In All Of Us*

287. Those who are absent from the conversation are the ones most full of shit.
    —Old English Proverb

288. It is better to be constipated in the company of the wise than to shit with fools.
    —Middle English Proverb

289. God gives the shits to those who have no toilet paper.
    —Pessimistic Spanish Proverb

290. Never trust the advice of someone who can't take a shit.
 —*Aesop's Paraphrased Fables*

291. I durst not laugh, for fear of opening my lips and receiving the bad air.
 —Sign on the door of Shakespeare's shithouse

292. He who would rise high should veil his shit with forms of wisdom.
 —Old Chinese Proverb

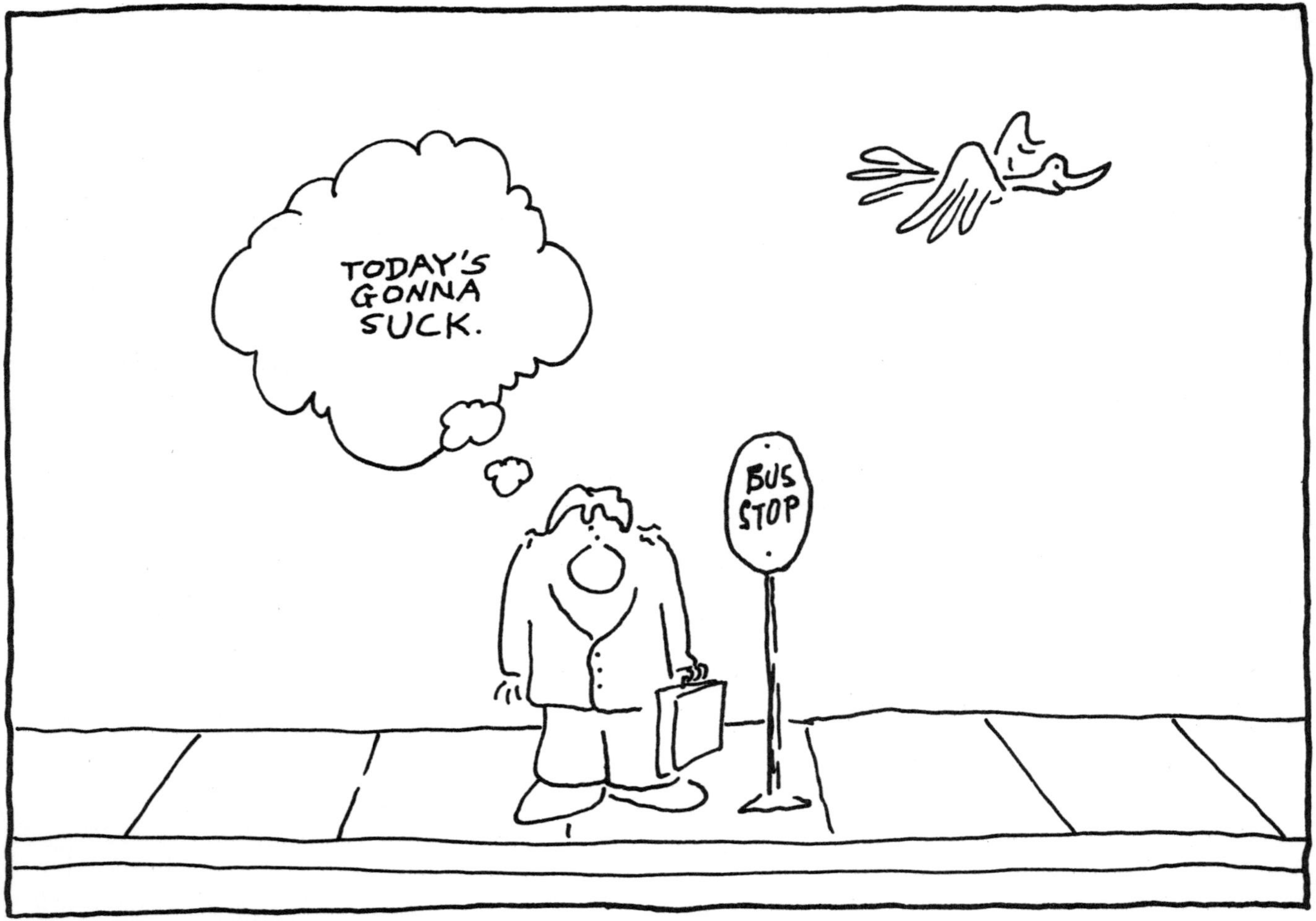
TODAY'S GONNA SUCK.
BUS STOP

293. From noble and common shit arises the same vile stink.
    —Old German Proverb

294. It is folly to hold the shithouse door open for a constipated man.
    —Old Chinese-German Proverb

295. Shit is a lie that makes us realize the truth.

296. We are all in the shitter, but some of us are looking up at stars.
    —Oscar Wilde, almost

· SHIT HAPPENS ·

297. He that lies down in shit will rise up with a bad smell.
　　—Old Latin Proverb

298. A good shit is one of the rare things that does not lead to doubt of god.
　　—*The Wisdom of Shit*

299. To keep shit in its place is to make all things beautiful.
　　—Close to what George Santayana said

300. Someone with too much to do will do something shitty.
　　—Platz's Platitude

301. One may have two good eyes and still step in shit.
     —Old Italian Proverb

302. Shitting is the reason man does not easily take himself for a god.
     —Nearly Nietzsche

303. Shitcan, as a noun 1: any receptacle into which shit drops 2: as a verb, to discard, get rid of, do away with, fire (from a job)

· SHIT HAPPENS ·

304. A shitty home remedy: if you want to clear your system out, sit on a piece of cheese and swallow a mouse.
—Johnny Carson

305. The camels shit, but the caravan moves on.
   —Old Egyptian Proverb

306. The wider any shit is spread, the thinner it gets.
   —The First Law of Diminishing Returns

307. Shitting is a very crude attempt to get into the rhythm of life.
   George Bernard Pshaw

308. A clean lid often hides a dirty shitter.
   —Old Bosnian Proverb

SHIT HAPPENS

309. He who digs a hole for another man's shit may fall into it himself.
    —Old Russian Proverb

310. Taking a shit is like gold in the morning, silver at noon, lead in the night.
    —*A Metallurgist Looks at Shit*

311. One cannot shit well if one has not dined well.
    —*A Fat Lover's Guide to Shitting*

...AND SO I KNEW IT WAS ALL OVER BETWEEN US WHEN I SMELLED SOMEONE ELSE'S SHIT ON HER NOSE.

·SHIT HAPPENS·

312. Crock of shit, an expression 1: any information deemed unreliable 2: a vessel filled with excrement

313. Many paths lead to the shithouse, but the smell is always the same.
    —Semi-old Chinese Proverb

314. Those who realize they're full of shit are not truly full of shit.
    —Semi-young Chinese Proverb

315. It is better to shit on your feet than to be constipated in the outhouse.
    —Rallying cry of the French Revolution

316. A good shit is a slow-ripening fruit.
   —*The Forgotten Words of Aristotle*

317. The worst things: to be in bed and sleep not, to want for one who comes not, to try to shit and shit not.
   —Found on the wall of a public toilet in Zimbabwe

318. A hurried shit has no blessing.
   —Old Swahili Proverb

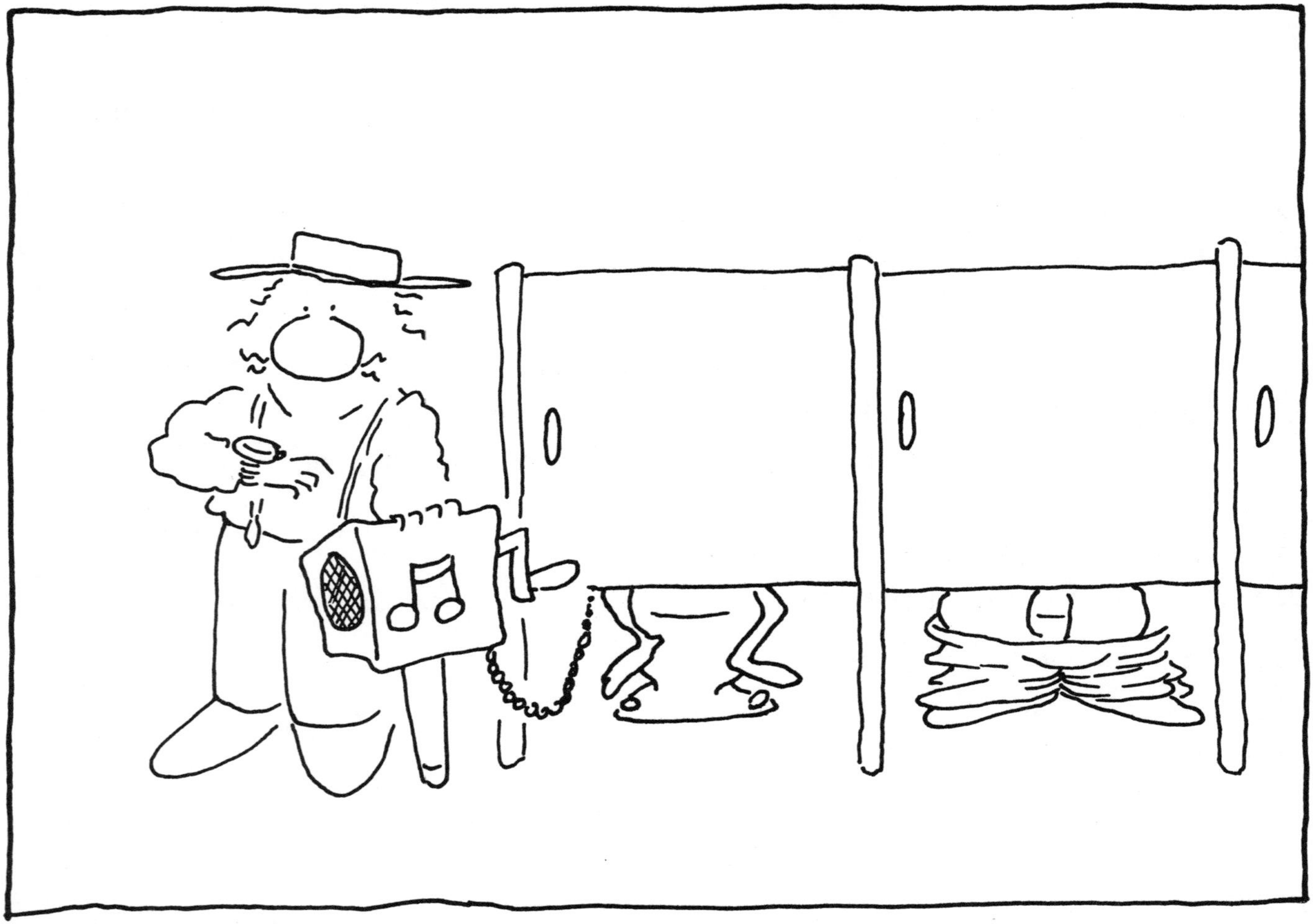

319. A pile of shit must prove itself shit at last, notwithstanding it being disguised as something other.
—What Sa'di wished he had said

320. Man was created on the sixth day so that he could not be boastful, since he came after dogshit in the order of creation.
—*The Apocryphal Palestinian Talmud*

321. Not to shit is bad; not to wish to shit is worse.
—Old Nigerian Proverb

322. Like a word, a shit, once let go cannot be called back.
—Thomas Fullofit

Shit Happens

323. Since shit rolls downhill, the wise keep an eye open on their uphill side.
     —Dusty's Directive: Part One

324. Since shit rolls downhill, the wiser keep well away from slopes.
     —Dusty's Directive: Part Two

325. Since shit rolls downhill, the wisest stay high.
     —Dusty's Directive: Part Three

326. To a Mormon: shit happens again and again and again.

· SHIT HAPPENS ·

327. Tough shit, an expression
1: bad luck 2: an angry comeback 3: a difficult bowel movement

328. The only time you'll need a plumber for the shitter is when you have diarrhea.
—Sixth Dictum of Pessimism

329. Whoever invented pay toilets should have the shit kicked out of them.
—Anonymous graffiti

330. Where there is no shit, there is no life.
—Original motto of the Explorers Club, later repealed by unanimous vote

331. Would it upset you terribly if I asked you to take your silly ass problem down the hall, per chance to find someone who really gives a shit?
　—Sylvester the Cat after another birdless day

332. After a satisfying shit, if you smile and the world smiles back, check to see if you left the door open.

333. Deep shit, an expression 1: a whole lot of trouble 2: what you'll find at the bottom of a well-used outhouse

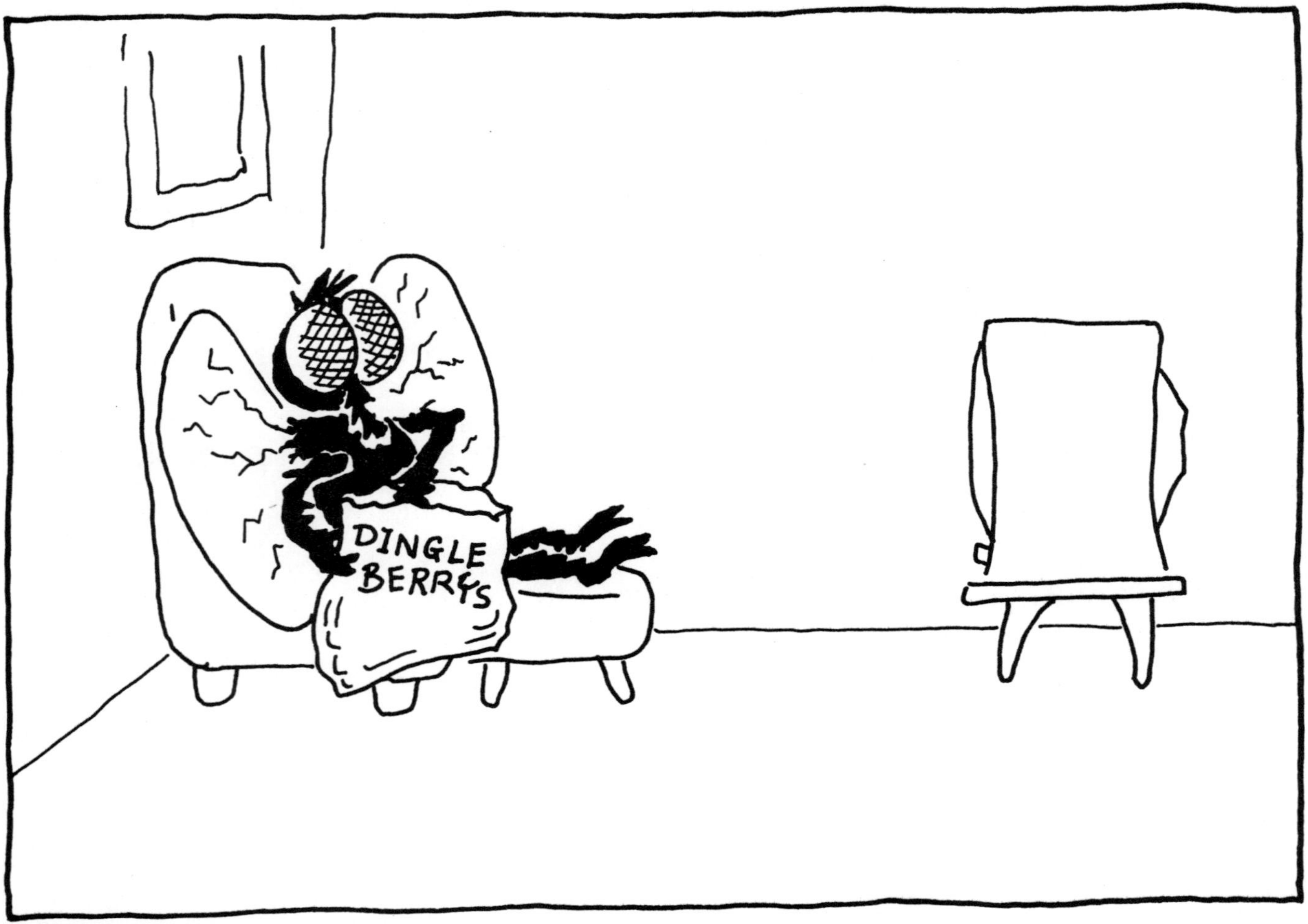
DINGLE
BERRYS

334. The trouble with getting into deep shit is that it usually starts out as fun.
—Daryl's Observation

335. Animal excreta smearing our language:
    1. Bullshit: untruth, exaggeration, nonsense.
    2. Chickenshit: coward, cowardly.
    3. Dogshit: dirty, rotten, ugly.
    4. Horseshit: lies, misdirected conversation.

336. Shit is like a train that's nearly always late.
—A commuter's comment

337. He who does not know his own shit will pretend he knows the shit of another.
—Old Kenyan Proverb

338. The most wasted day is that in which we have not shit.
—*The Bowels of Chamfort*

339. Laugh, and the world laughs with you; shit, and you shit alone.
—With apologies to Ella Wheeler Wilcox

· SHIT HAPPENS ·

340. Let your settling on the toilet seat decrease, not increase, your irritability.
—*Articles of the Good Shit Club*, Number Fourteen

· SHIT HAPPENS ·

341. To a Unitarian: what is this shit?

342. A shlemiehl is someone who lands on his back with his face in shit.
   —Old Yiddish definition

343. Shit is, after all, the gift of oneself.

344. The more violent the shit, the more violent the sound.
   —Old Australian Proverb

345. The great tragedy of life in not that people perish, but that they sometimes can't take a shit.
—W. Somerset Moan

346. However well-made the outhouse, there's still shit at the bottom of it.
—Old Tibetan Proverb

347. (The) shits, a noun 1: a less-than-appealing situation 2: diarrhea, runs, trots, Montezuma's revenge, etc.

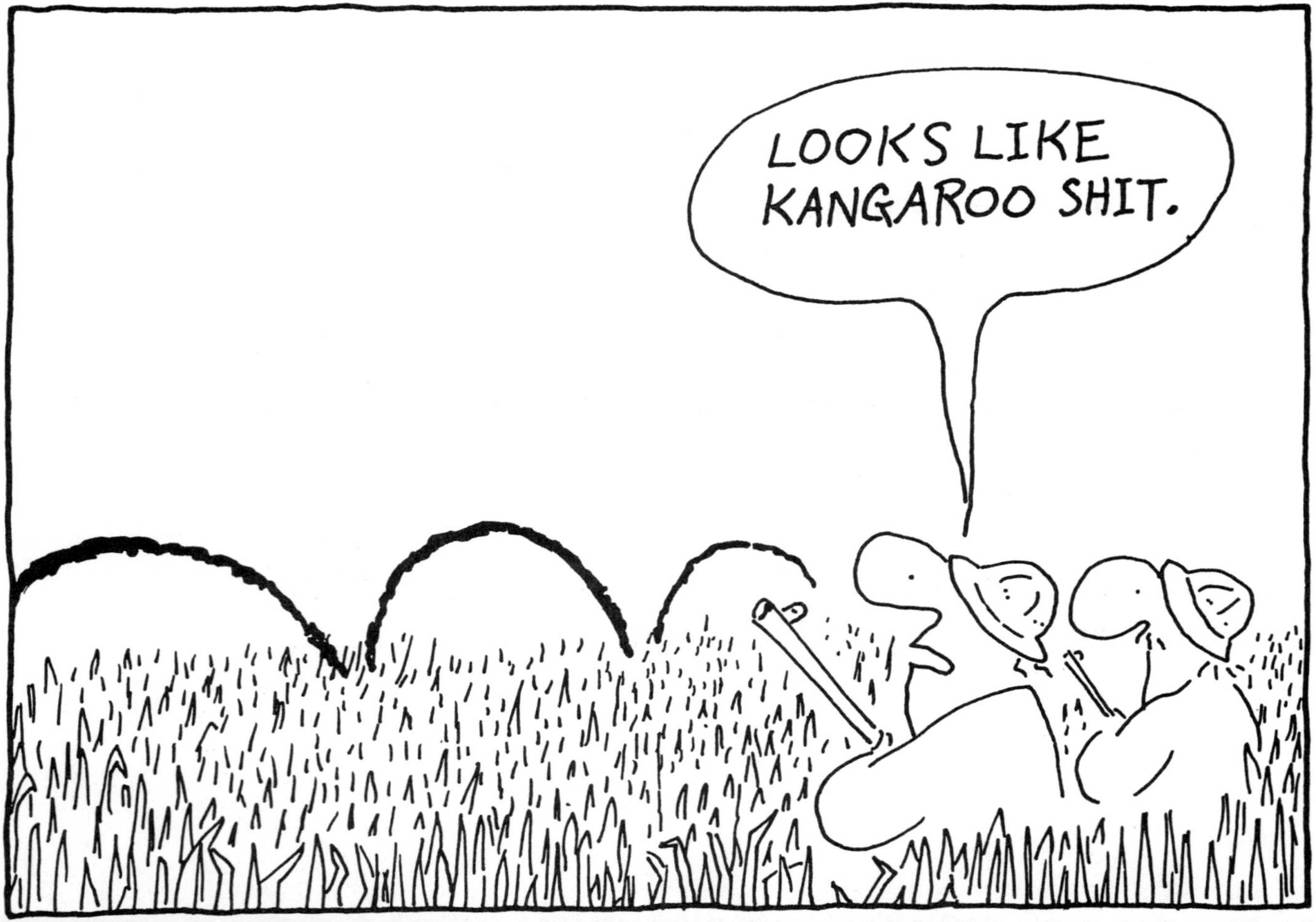
LOOKS LIKE KANGAROO SHIT.

· SHIT HAPPENS ·

348. No, really, try it. It just looks like shit.
—The origin of April Fool's Day

· SHIT HAPPENS ·

349. Shitology, a noun, a medical term the study of any shit except your own

350. When opportunity knocks, you'll be taking a shit.
    —Seventh Dictum of Pessimism

351. Shit is cheap because supply exceeds demand.

352. Shit the bed, an expression 1: to mess up an otherwise ok situation 2: to mess up the place where you sleep

353. To a Rastafarian: let's smoke this shit!

354. Zachary's thirteen-month-old opinion: poopy happens.

SHIT HAPPENS

355. Clean diapers are the best place for poopy to happen.
   —Corollary to Zachary's Opinion

356. Any shitty idea can be worded in an appealing way.
   —Carey's Canon

357. Any appealing idea can be worded in a shitty way.
   —Corollary to Carey's Canon

358. Pride is when you start believing your own shit.
   —Amy Jo's Reflection

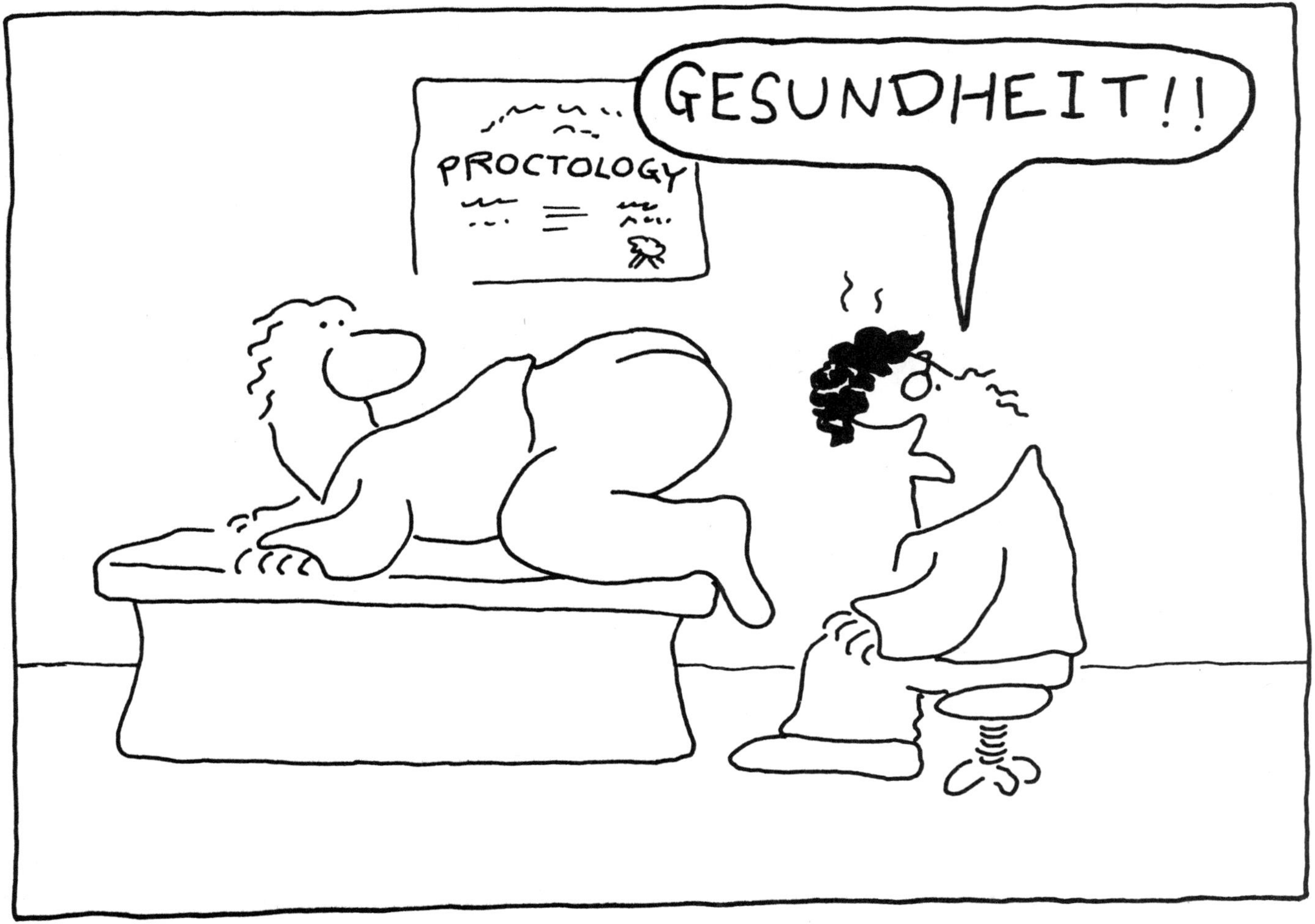
GESUNDHEIT!!
PROCTOLOGY

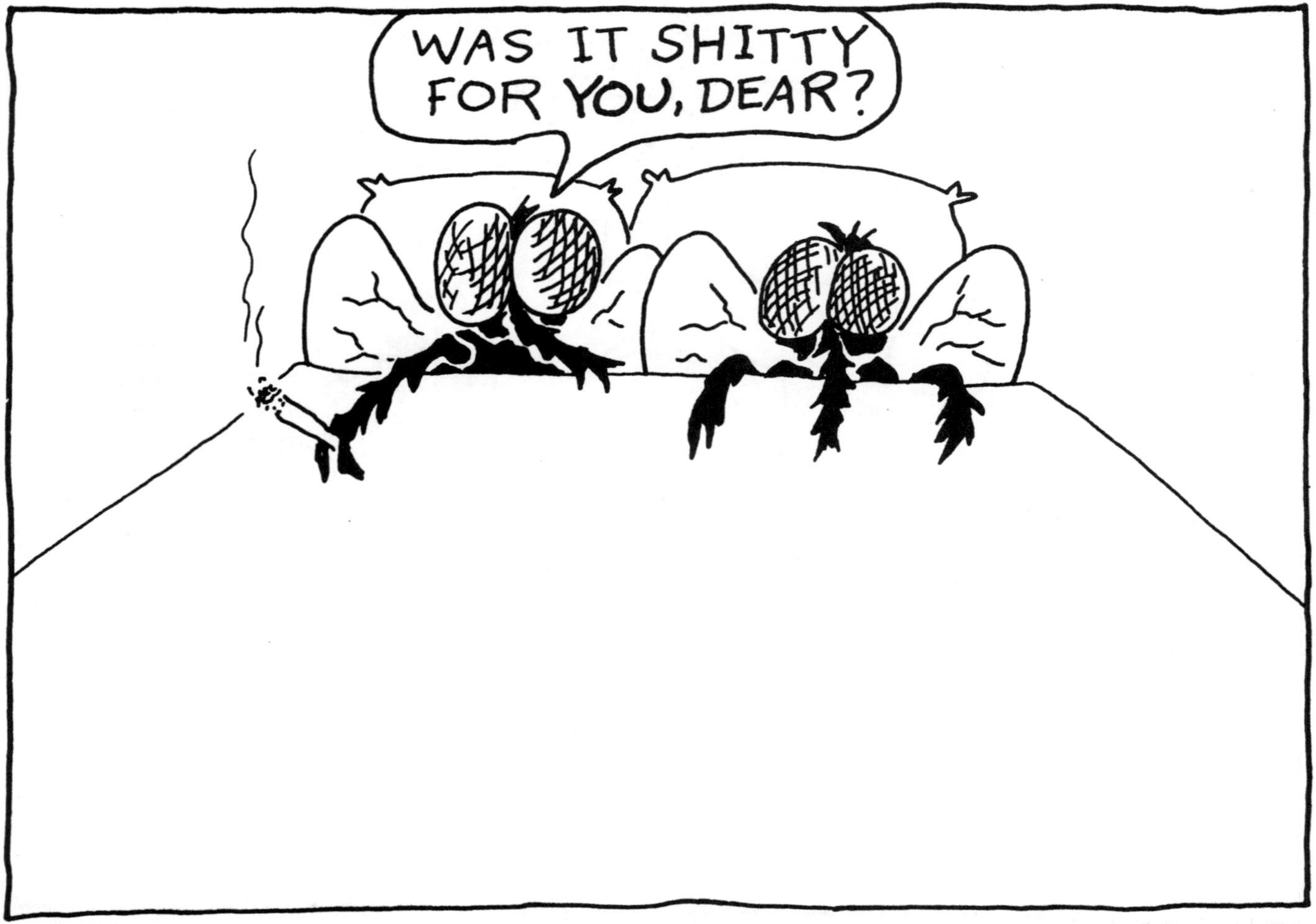
WAS IT SHITTY FOR YOU, DEAR?

· SHIT HAPPENS ·

359. I am convinced shitting is the great secret of life.
 —Anonymous constipated philosopher

· SHIT HAPPENS ·

360. All places are alike, and every piece of earth is fit to take a shit.
 —Very Old Ashanti Proverb

361. Like hatred, shit must be articulated or, like hatred, it will produce a disturbing internal malaise.
 —Something like what George Jean Nathan said

362. Be sure your shit will find you out.
 —The Gospel According to Shit 4:1

363. We are punished by our shit, not for it.
 —*On Life and Shit*

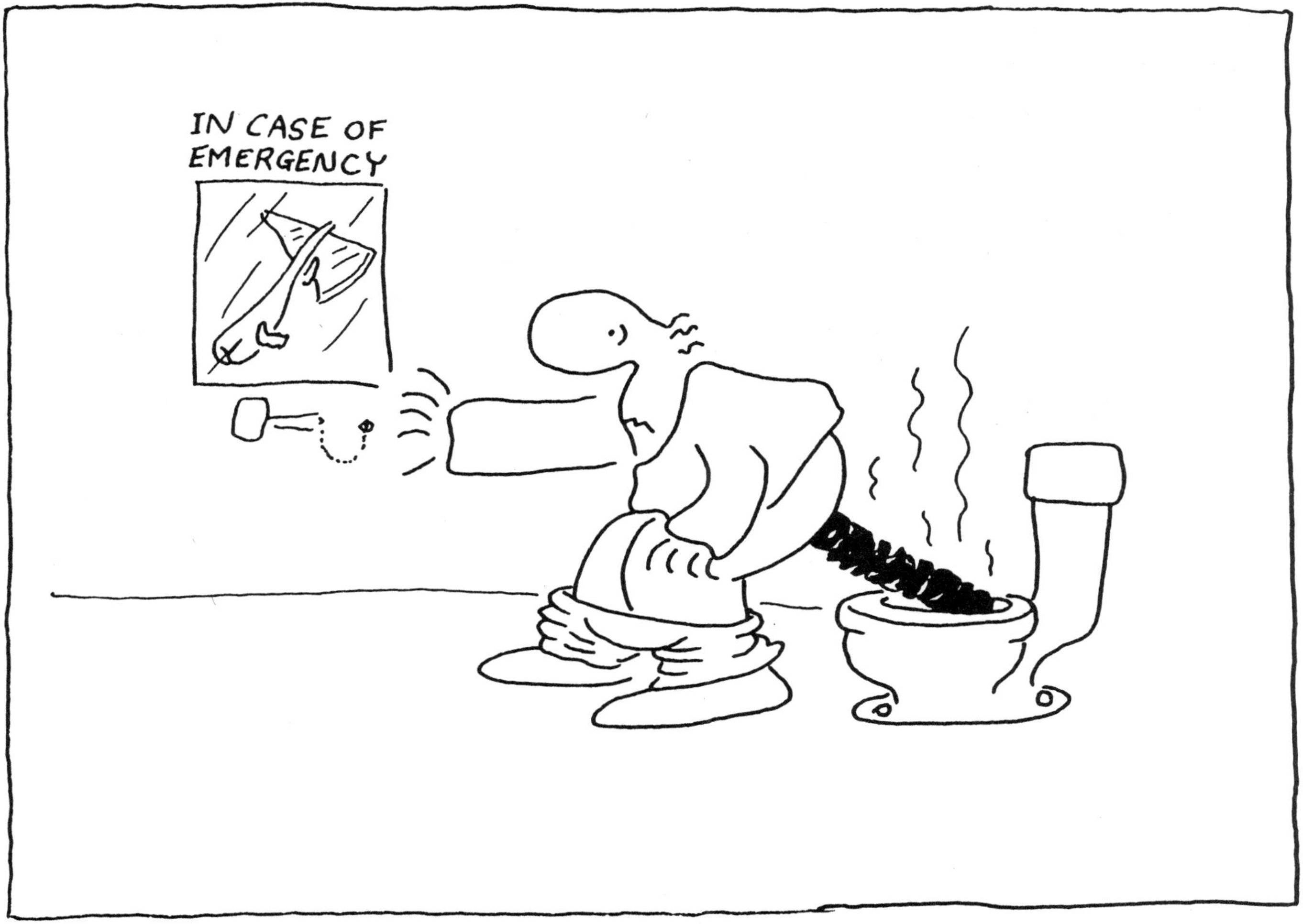
IN CASE OF
EMERGENCY

· SHIT HAPPENS ·

364. After all is said and done, there's a lot of shit been said and done.
    —McInaney's Maxim

365. Shit: the end result.

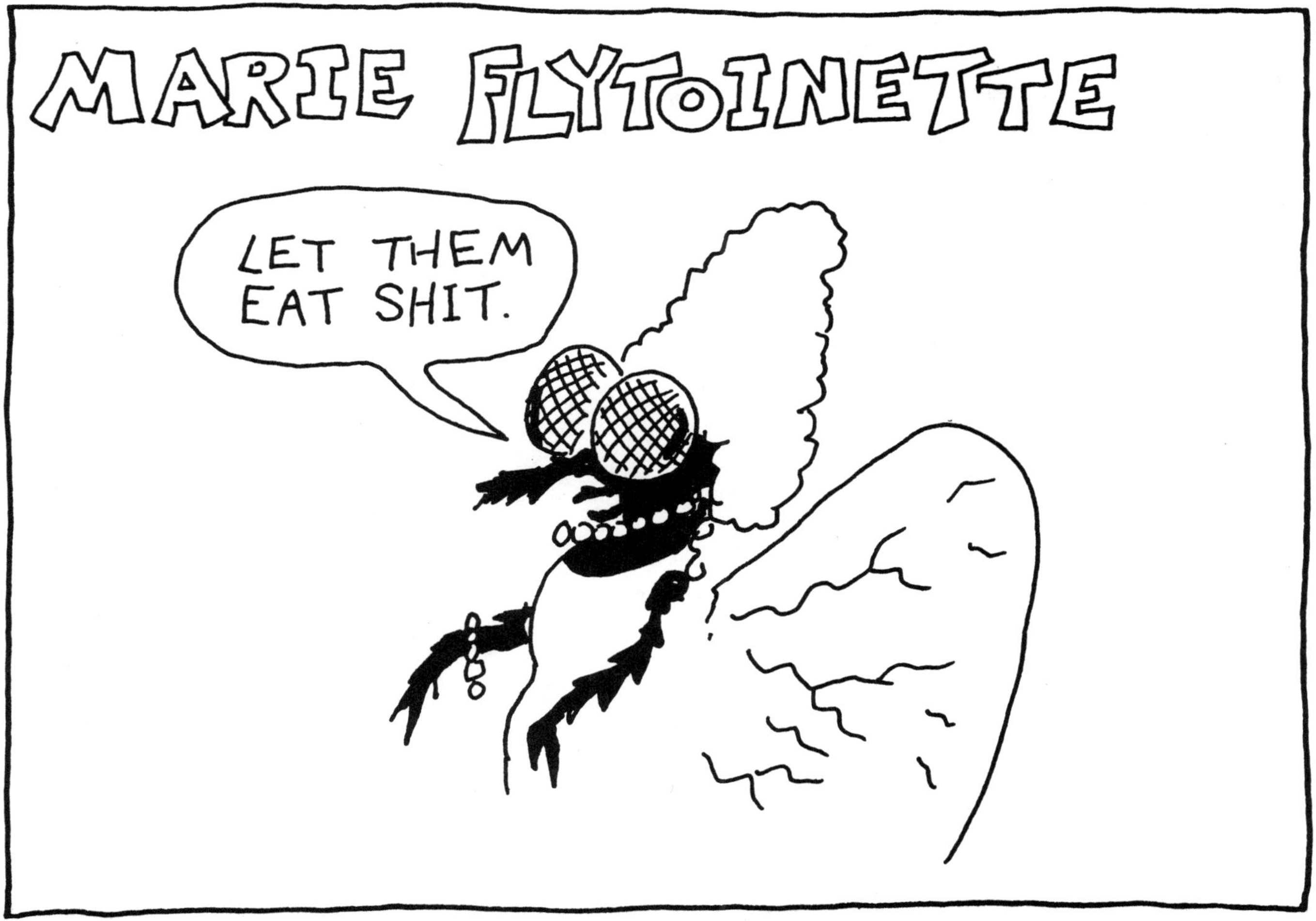
MARIE FLYTOINETTE
LET THEM EAT SHIT.

THE PARKERS' DOG GOES ON PAPER!!! THE BAXTERS' DOG GOES ON PAPER!!! THE JONES' DOG,...